MW01634369

Praise for
Grace Upon Grace

"As a friend, fan, and former neighbor of David Cottrell, I'm honored to recommend him to you. His books have touched countless thousands of people worldwide. I am confident that this work will exceed them all. David gleans wisdom from his own journey and, in doing so, invites us to examine our own."

 – Max Lucado
  Pastor and *New York Times* best-selling author
  Author of *Unshakable Hope*

"David is one of my all-time favorite authors and people. His heartfelt raw stories of real life within this book give hope to us all. Read it and be soaked through and through with grace."

 – David L. Cook, Ph.D.
  Author/executive producer of *Seven Days in Utopia*

"David has been a coach, mentor, spiritual adviser, and trusted friend of mine for over 30 years. I have walked with him through many of the experiences that he shares in this book and can attest that he has faced life's challenges head on with consistent prayer, wisdom, and discernment. He has taught me to find grace within every blessing, trial, and loss as we navigate through life. You will discover the same in *Grace Upon Grace*."

 – Tod Taylor
  Managing director
  FedEx

"*Grace Upon Grace* is a fascinating read about an ordinary person who God has used in extraordinary ways. David reveals his life story and guides you through his times of personal joy and suffering and business success and failures. Read this book. David's story will inspire you to become the person you want to be."

> – Pat Williams
> Orlando Magic founder and senior vice president
> Author of *Character Carved in Stone*

"It's one thing to know David as the ultimate professional that he is. Reading his life's story of WHO he is at his very core makes this book come alive. This back story shows HOW David has demonstrated his faith and core values as he built his successful career. David's character is a testament that living authentically can not only result in business success – but in life's fulfillment."

> – Valerie Sokolosky
> Fox News contributor and author of *Do It Right!*

"Some books can change your career and others can change your life. This book does both! David Cottrell has inspired me personally and elevated me professionally since the day we met in 2003. If reading this book is your only chance to meet David Cottrell, consider it a chance of a lifetime to learn from my trusted friend, mentor, and business partner. His struggles are genuine and relatable, and his lessons are practical and encouraging. By the time you finish his engaging story, you will view David as your trusted friend, mentor, and business partner. So, give yourself some Grace and read it today!"

> – Lee J. Colan, Ph.D.
> Author, *Sticking to It*

"David Cottrell is my friend and mentor. His newest book, *Grace Upon Grace,* contains important lessons that will help you maneuver through tough business situations and heart-wrenching personal challenges. You will be inspired by this Christian man who shows us that God's grace sustains us no matter what."

> – Lorraine Grubbs
> Former director of employment
> Southwest Airlines

"When I asked David for his primary motivation in writing this book, he told me it was for his family. What a noble assignment to chronicle your journey so your family knows your whole story and, consequently, an important piece of theirs. After I read it, I was immediately convinced it is for everyone. The story is uniquely David's, but the principles he shares in each of the 16 chapters are transferable to us all. If you and I apply the nuggets of wisdom contained within these pages, it will take us places we want to go and we will like who we are when we get there … people bathed in God's grace."

> – Randy Frazee
> Pastor and author of *The Heart of the Story*

Grace Upon Grace

My Story

David Cottrell

Unless otherwise indicated, all Scripture quotations are taken from the HOLY BIBLE, NEW INTERNATIONAL VERSION®, copyright © 1973, 1978, 1984, by International Bible Society. Used by permission of Zondervan Publishing House. All rights reserved.

Scripture quotations marked "KJV" are taken from the Holy Bible, King James Version.

The "NIV" and "New International Version" trademarks are registered in the United States Patent and Trademark Office by International Bible Society. Use of either trademark requires the permission of International Bible Society.

Inquiries regarding permission for use of the material contained in this book should be addressed to:

CornerStone Leadership Institute
P.O. Box 764087
Dallas, TX 75376
972-298-8377

Paperback ISBN: 978-0-9961469-8-2
Hard Cover ISBN: 978-0-9961469-9-9
Printed in the United States of America. 10 9 8 7 6 5 4 3 2 1

Credits

Cover photo:	Jason Risner Photography, RisnerPhoto.com
Editor:	Stephen Douglas Williford, StephenWilliford.com
Copy editor:	Kathleen Green, Positively Proofed, info@PositivelyProofed.com
Design, art direction, and production:	Melissa Farr, Back Porch Creative, info@backporchcreative.com

Table of Contents

Grace Upon Grace

---

*From his abundance we have all received
one gracious blessing after another.*
– John 1:16 (NLT)

Grace upon grace. That is the best way to describe my life.

I have heard and read about many people describing themselves as being "self-made." That is something that I cannot comprehend or understand. There is nothing "self-made" about me. My life has been blessed with a series of one gracious blessing after another, just like it was written in the Gospel of John about 2,000 years ago.

God's grace has encompassed my life. It has been like a soft blanket that covered me when I was afraid. It has protected me from my faults and blunders. It has forgiven me when I made mistakes. It has embraced me when I hurt. It has saturated me with peace in times of suffering. His grace has shaped and strengthened me.

Never in my wildest dreams could I have imagined the twists and turns that have happened to me. It is inconceivable how His grace has sustained and prospered me, even when I did nothing to earn it. His grace abundantly gifted me with wonderful parents, two incredible wives, three children, three stepchildren, five children in-law, 10 grandchildren, numerous loyal friends, and the ideal jobs that were lined up perfectly for me to become who I am.

I have discovered that the only way anyone could understand how life's events – whether pain and suffering or joy – are woven to create a tapestry of a person's life is to take the time to reflect. Documenting my life in this book has not been easy. In fact, it was awkward and uncomfortable. The questions that I had to keep asking myself and answering were: *Why would anyone want to read about my backstory? Is it important? Does anyone care? Is it worth the effort?*

My first response to each of those questions was that it really doesn't matter. Oh, there may be some interested readers, I reflected, but the truth is that I needed to understand my own backstory. It is important to me. I care. It is worth my effort.

Well, that was my first thought. But as I began to put these moments of my life on the page, another thought emerged. "Maybe there are some of my life experiences that can be translated into life lessons for others." I hope you'll consider this not only a book about my life but about how these words might help you in your life.

You have a story, too. In fact, there are experiences described in this book that you may be living today. There are chapters in my story that may become chapters in your story in the future. *Grace Upon Grace* exposes my life experiences so you can laugh and cry with me. But, more importantly, it is for you to draw strength and inspiration when you are in the midst of a personal storm in your life. And, I hope it will be a reminder for you to celebrate grace during your time of peace and joy. My greatest desire is that my story will make you more acutely aware of your own story and all of your gracious blessings, regardless of your current circumstances.

As of this writing, I am 65 years old. I don't think that God is finished with me yet. With His grace, I may live many more years so I can add more chapters to this book. In fact, I am not so sure if there may be another entire book based on my future years.

Regardless of how many more pages remain in my life, this will always be the story of my first 65. Six-and-a-half decades of successes and failures, breakthroughs and heartbreaks, joy and suffering.

The chapters of the book flow sequentially, beginning with my heritage and ending with today.

Each chapter ends with some of my personal thoughts about the lessons I learned during that time of my life and how those lessons may apply to you.

You may want to skip chapters, depending on your situation. That is okay.

- If you are working through a health crisis, you may want to begin at the *Grace of Suffering*.

- You may want to go to the *Grace of Perseverance* and *Mind-blowing Grace* if you are wrestling with starting a business or struggling in your business.

> ✦ You may choose to start at the *Grace of Dignity* if you are helping a friend or relative through their end of life.
>
> ✦ If you are wondering about your hope for the future, you may want to jump directly to the *Grace of Today*.
>
> ✦ Or, if you are in the mood for a couple of wonderful love stories, go to the *Grace of Love* and the *Grace of Loving Again*.

The pages that you hold in your hand are my memories. While investing your time by reading this book, please hang on and enjoy the ride with me. My desire is that you will sense that each word written in *Grace Upon Grace* is a reflection of my gratitude and amazement for how everything worked together to form my life. It is lined with memories of love, loss, and pain. Those memories help to remind me that every moment of my life, even my most painful moments, have contributed to make me who I am.

I hope you will be inspired by this story of a boy from Arkansas whose life has been filled with an abundance of grace upon grace.

one

Grace of My Heritage

From the Backwoods of Arkansas

*We can chart our future clearly and wisely only when we know
the path which has led to the present.*
— ADLAI STEVENSON

One of my most pleasant discoveries in writing this book was
that I developed a better understanding of my heritage. I had
fond, loving memories of my parents and grandparents, but
I had never taken the time to look back and reflect upon the
positive impact that they had on every area of my life.

My ancestors taught me how to work hard and enjoy living.
They taught me that being joyful did not require wealth,
possessions, or prosperity. They
didn't have any of that. They taught
me to be grateful for the little things
that many times I had a tendency to
overlook. As I look back, I can see
how they were incredible stewards of
the graces they had been provided.

Mom and Dad

I thank God for the grace of my
heritage.

Mom

My mother, Mary Lee McClain, was raised in Fordyce, Arkansas. Fordyce is a small rural community in the south central part of Arkansas. It is best known for being the home of Paul "Bear" Bryant. Before becoming one of the greatest college football coaches of all time, Bryant was a defensive lineman and offensive end for the Fordyce Redbugs.

Mom's parents, Ragus and Betty McClain, lived their entire married life in a log cabin where my mom was born. I am not sure how my grandparents wound up in Fordyce, but I am positive that they never saw many bright lights outside the city limits of Fordyce.

Both of my mom's parents passed when I was young, but I have some vivid memories of them. I remember Maw Maw chasing chickens in her yard, catching one, wringing its neck, plucking its feathers, and within an hour serving it up as fried chicken. I witnessed with my own eyes what it meant to be "running around like a chicken with its head cut off." She would also skin and fry squirrels that we shot in the woods close to their house. My clogged arteries later in life may have had its beginnings with my grandmother's cooking.

I remember my grandmother and Mag – her full-time helper who was considered a part of the family – scrubbing clothes on a washboard by hand and then putting the clothes through a manual wringer before hanging them up to dry. Most young people today probably do not know where the phrase "put you through the wringer" came from, but I do. When my grandparents bought an electric wringer from the local hardware store, it was a really big deal.

I remember walking about 50 yards – in the cold, hot, rain, or whatever the season presented – to the outhouse and frequently seeing a snake along the way. It was a great day when they had plumbing built into their house.

They had a phone mounted on the wall in the hall leading to their bedroom. The phone had a crank that you had to wind up to connect to an operator, who would then connect you to the person you were trying to call. My aunt was a telephone operator. She knew everything that was happening in Fordyce. Telephone operators were the social media of their day.

My grandparents' telephone was connected with several others, which was called a "party line." Each home's phone had a distinct ring, like one short ring and two long rings, so you would know who the caller was attempting to reach. The party line had nothing to do with partying … other than you could listen to what some of your neighbors were talking about.

My grandparents worked hard. Paw Paw worked at the lumber yard until he died at age 63. I was eight years old when he passed. Two things that I remember about him were that he would come home from work and saddle up Prince, who I recall being a huge horse, and then walk with me riding Prince around his property. I also remember him making homemade shaving cream in a white ceramic coffee cup and splashing the warm cream on my face and pretending that he was shaving me.

Maw Maw eventually became blind from diabetes, but I remember her quilting as though she was reading braille in the "den." Someone would hang the material from the four corners of the room and she would quilt until all four corners met. Maw Maw passed when she was 76 years old.

My grandparents are buried side-by-side outside of Fordyce. The inscription on their tombstone reads, "A life like theirs left a record sweet for memory to dwell upon." And it does.

Mom was a shy redhead. Until she married my dad when she was 19 years old, she probably had not traveled more than 30 miles away from Fordyce. As a young lady, she worked in the local Western Auto Store where she caught the eye of one of her customers, who was to become her husband. After a few intentional visits to the auto store, my dad – then a "mature" 23-year-old – finally got the nerve to ask her for a date.

After a brief courtship, they were married in my mom's family home in Fordyce on June 29, 1918. That log cabin home is still standing and is now an Arkansas historical preserved home.

My grandparents' house

When Mom and Dad met, Daddy had already dedicated his life to Christ and was preaching in several churches in rural Arkansas. He was the pastor of three churches at once. He would lead services at one church on Sunday morning, another on Sunday evening, and another on Wednesday night. Sometimes they would have "dinner on the grounds" between the Sunday services. They would sing, pray, preach, eat, pray, and sing. It was quite a day.

Those old rural churches did not have much money being put into the offering plate. In fact, many times in lieu of money, Dad would be "paid" chickens, pigs, or whatever fruits and vegetables were in season. My mom and dad frequently talked about how they enjoyed those early marriage challenges together side-by-side.

She was a great partner for my dad. Daddy was color blind and she would lay his neatly ironed clothes on the bed for him every day. She loved him.

Mom could also take control of my dad when needed. One time in the late 1950s, while living in Pine Bluff, Arkansas, my parents did not have enough money for Mom to make my two sisters new Easter dresses. She cried and prayed for God to provide. That spring, Oscar Mayer was having a promotion. If the Oscar Mayer man knocked on your door and you had one of their products, you would win a cash prize. Mom had safely stored two Oscar Mayer wieners in the freezer while waiting patiently for the Oscar Mayer man to knock on their door. One Sunday night after church, my dad declared that it was time to eat those wieners and took them out of the freezer. Right before he was about to take his first bite, mom grabbed them from him and scolded him … *"Those wieners are for the Oscar Mayer man; you can't have them!"* Laughing and trying to satisfy his wife, Daddy reluctantly placed the two wieners back in the freezer. The very next morning while mom was cleaning the house and singing (more appropriately, making a joyful noise) her favorite song, "God Will Take Care of You," the Oscar Mayer man knocked on the door. She handed over her two frozen wieners and the Oscar Mayer man presented her with $40 cash. That was plenty of money for her to buy enough material to make new Easter outfits for her girls.

Mom grew up during the Depression. She lived her life based on faith, hard work, and joyful love. She was the sweetest person I have ever known. During my school years, I worked each summer mowing cemetery lawns, painting, and working on a framing crew building houses. She would rise early every day and fix my lunch for me to take to work. At least once a week she would fry three pieces of chicken for me to take. The smell of my mother frying chicken at 6:30 a.m. is an aroma that is permanently ingrained in my memory. Every day after work, I would come home to another pleasing aroma, the clean fragrance of Pine-Sol after she cleaned our house that day.

Mother demanded that I work hard. She would not let me play until all work was completed. Many days I wanted to go play football, baseball, or basketball with the neighborhood guys, but I would have to finish my piano lesson. I hated that.

She taught me how to have simple faith and depend on God's direction in my life. She did not lecture us a whole lot, but she shared some common wisdom that has stuck with me all of my life. Some of her favorites were from Scripture: "*Be sure your sins will find you out*" quoted from Numbers 32:33 and "*When the ox is in the ditch, you have to get it out*" from Luke 14:5. She even quoted Shakespeare's "*This too shall pass*" when encouraging me that no matter how tough the situation, it was not permanent. She taught me how to be happy and accept any situation with dignity.

Mom was a woman of grace and peace. Even in her final days when she was suffering from Alzheimer's, she maintained her pleasant countenance and never wavered from always ensuring our family that "I am right where I ought to be."

Dad

My dad, Ralph Cottrell, was born on November 24, 1921. His parents were Sanders and Ida Cottrell. My grandmother was a widow; her first husband passed away at a relatively young age.

Dad had a trailer load of siblings. My grandmother had quite an imagination with names. Dad's half brothers and sister's names were: Otis, Leona, Ruby, Blanche, Adrian, Gordon, Taylor, Bruce, and Ollin Ray – who died shortly after birth. Their last name was Reddin. Then after marrying my grandfather, she came up with some more grand names: Norman, Thelbert, and my dad, Ralph, were the Cottrell boys. They rounded out an even dozen children for my grandmother.

Dad and his two brothers

The Cottrell family was dirt poor. They lived in the backwoods of Arkansas. My dad was born and raised in Hampton, Arkansas, a town of about 1,000 at the time. Hampton was the county seat of Calhoun County, also known as Hogskin County. Back in the day, there were a number of hogs running the river bottoms of Calhoun County. People from surrounding counties would come there to kill and skin the hogs. The hogskins were left hanging on a fence and the dressed hog was taken back to the family for food. The nickname "Hogskin County" has remained through the years. Even today you can visit the Hogskin Holidays Festival and participate in a rodeo, watch the Hogskin Hunnies mounted equestrian drill team perform, listen to the Hammin' It Up Band, and then enjoy the main attraction of the Cummins Prison Band.

Calhoun County was, and still is, the least-populated county in the state of Arkansas. The 632 square miles of Calhoun County have about 5,000 residents. Trees outnumbered residents probably 1,000-to-1.

Even with all the challenges my dad's parents faced, they must have worked on doing the most important things really well. Out of my grandmother's eight boys, four became ministers. The other boys each had respectable careers, including one becoming a sheriff and another was the county agriculture commissioner. My dad's half sisters were successful as well.

In the end, my grandmother's tombstone read: "She hath done what she could."

My dad was not born with a silver spoon in his mouth. When I describe his home as "backwoods," your imagination is probably far more civilized than reality. Hogskin County was in the back of the backwoods. His parents were farmers, and all of their children were raised to work hard.

Back in those days, a college education was beyond imagination for the Reddin and Cottrell kids. Receiving a high school diploma was the ultimate education for them. Dad earned his high school diploma, finished some college work, and attended a small seminary.

At the age of 17, he was called to the ministry and was ordained when he was 19 years old. For the next 60 years, until the week he died at age 79, the most comfortable place for him was in the church leading his congregation. He was passionate about Christ, and his sermons reflected such. The longer he preached, the louder he got – sometimes pounding the pulpit to get his point across.

Dad was a great orator. He studied diligently. He was always prepared to preach. I don't think he ever just went through the motions. A large part of my life was spent in church – Sunday morning, Sunday night, Wednesday night, and when we had revivals, every night.

One of my most vivid memories of my dad's church leadership was in 1963. We lived in Laurel, Mississippi, when racial tensions were at their peak. Laurel was right smack dab in the middle of the fight for segregation/integration. A church was burned down not far from our church. The young adult Freedom Riders were murdered less than 50 miles from where we lived. The times were tense.

My dad was the pastor at Parkview Baptist Church, which of course was all white. He loved Laurel and Parkview but did not love the way the city and church were divided on the issue of race relations. One Sunday night, there was a church meeting to develop a plan in case of demonstration or integration at our church. There was some passionate discussion. Several of the influential members of the church were thought to be active in the Ku Klux Klan.

My dad's position was black and white – we are all God's children and should be treated as such. Others thought that no one of a different color should walk through the doors. The debate raged, and my dad offered an alternative. He proposed that the church allow them to worship with us but have a special section where they would be seated. Many of his parishioners did not like that. In fact, they began to put his love for Laurel and Parkview to a real test. Finally, after about a year of agony, he resigned.

Through it all, he stood his ground and taught me the lesson of always doing the right thing.

My dad continued to do well, but I don't think he ever completely got over the poor treatment from a powerful few in Laurel. He went on to lead several other churches and continued to lead many to Christ. During his twilight years, he founded the Ministers Benevolent Society, which was created to help pastors who did not have a retirement plan. That may have been his defining moment and part of his legacy that continues today. He also was the author of *Go Ye and Teach, The New You,* and *Sermon Outlines Through the Bible.*

Daddy also taught me the game of golf. He was not a great golfer, but he loved to hack the ball around. He was a right-handed golfer with an unusual stance. He would position his right foot about 12 inches or so behind his front left foot. He looked pretty funny, but he would hit the ball reasonably well. His golf handicap probably never broke 18 in his life. However, he loved to play. When he made a par, he was thrilled. He used the game of golf to teach me many life lessons, including patience (I was not a good student of that lesson), integrity, accepting the consequences of my choices, and that you have to finish every hole regardless of how many strokes it took you to get there.

He also taught me to be proud of our name. Even though we were not in the same economic status as most of my friends, I was always proud to say I was a Cottrell. As an adult when I went to him for advice, it seems as though most of the time he told me "Remember, Rome wasn't built in a day" or "Well, what do you think is the right thing to do?" To be patient and do the right thing were his most common and important lessons for me.

In 1978, Dad was among the first generation of people to have heart bypass surgery. His surgeon was Dr. Denton Cooley, one of the early pioneers in heart surgery. After my dad's successful surgery, he never experienced any further heart issues until early Sunday morning, April 9, 2001. On that day, he awoke in excruciating pain. He woke my mom and asked her to drive him to the hospital. By the time they arrived, his pain had subsided.

His cardiologist scheduled an arteriogram for the following day to see what damage had been done and to determine what course of recovery would be required. It was one of the very few times in his life that Dad canceled preaching. When I visited him in the hospital that Sunday afternoon, he was acting normal and still had his sense of humor. No one, including the doctors, comprehended the seriousness of what had happened.

On Monday, during the arteriogram, he had another heart attack and never regained consciousness. He died on April 11, the Tuesday before Easter in 2001.

My dad lived life to the fullest. In his final week, he was prepared to preach – his Bible was open on his desk to the passage that would be his sermon topic that Sunday. Two days before, on Friday, he played golf. He was able to see, talk, and laugh with all his family on the Sunday after his heart attack. He had surgery on Monday. He died on Tuesday and his funeral was on Good Friday. If he were to have scripted his final week, I bet it would have been exactly the same.

On Easter Sunday, all of our family worshipped together at his church. There has not been a day that has passed since his death that I have not thought of my father.

Your Grace of Heritage Applied

I hope that your heritage provides you many of the same sweet memories as mine. I was raised in a loving home that provided me a solid foundation. If you feel the same, I hope you will take the time to share those memories with your family. Write them down. Talk about them. Ask those around you how they remember certain facts of your life. It will lead to some interesting conversations with your loved ones.

I have several friends who did not grow up in a loving home. In fact, they grew up in a toxic family environment of hate, abuse, addictions, and unfathomable circumstances.

If your situation is like that, I hope that you will try to look beyond your past pain and toward the legacy that you want to leave your family. You have been given the grace to answer for yourself two important questions: *Who do you want to become?* and *What legacy do you want to leave?*

I have a friend who decided that he was not going to be a victim of his past. He was raised in a situation that was so bad that the details are not appropriate to be printed. He broke out of that environment and became a successful, positive person. He became the person that he wanted to become, rather than the person that he was tracking to become. His road wasn't easy. In fact, it was more difficult than you can imagine.

If you decide to become the person you want to become instead of the person you are tracking to become, your road will not be easy, either. I hope you will consider unlocking the chains of your past, move beyond blaming anyone for the pain inflicted upon you, and begin becoming the person that you want to be.

Your past does not have a future, but you do. You can begin living a positive legacy right now. I hope you will.

Two

Grace of New Experiences

Early Years – Moving Around

When I was a kid my parents moved a lot,
but I always found them.

— RODNEY DANGERFIELD

My story began on October 4, 1953, at 3:15 a.m. in Room 3 of a 20-bed hospital in Nashville, Arkansas. I weighed in at a healthy nine pounds and four ounces.

My first grace was being born into a family of wonderful parents and two loving sisters. My sisters were not too loving at first, though. When they found out that a baby brother was coming into their world, they were not happy. In fact, when my dad took my sisters, Sherry and Evelyn, to see me at the hospital, both of the girls turned their heads and refused to look at me. There were tears, but not tears of joy.

My dad was excited that he had a boy. At least that is what my mom told me. He stayed with mom at the hospital until it was time for him to go to the local radio station where he had a Sunday morning radio program. He proudly declared on live radio for all to hear that he was the father of a baby boy. After the radio broadcast, he drove his 1940 Plymouth directly to Immanuel Baptist Church and delivered his Sunday morning sermon.

Nashville, Arkansas, is situated in the foothills of the Ouachita Mountains. The city is famous for two things – mouth-watering, large, yellow-fleshed peaches and being the home of the first Dillard's department store, which opened in Nashville in 1938.

In 1953, the population of Nashville was about 3,000 residents. It was not exactly a thriving metropolis. The drought of 1952 and 1953 had taken a toll on the peach-farming industry. Times were tough. The congregation of Immanuel Baptist had been devastated by the drought. There were weeks when the church offering did not cover the utility bills – much less the young pastor's salary. However, my mom and dad were able to keep their kids healthy and clothed, and provided for our needs.

We never had much money, but you could depend on our home being filled with love. On any given day you could hear my mom or dad singing "Amazing Grace," "Great is Thy Faithfulness," "Love Lifted Me," "How Great Thou Art," and many other hymns that lifted their spirits when times were tough.

Like most families of pastors of small Baptist churches, we moved frequently. Everywhere that we lived, we were surrounded by Methodists, Presbyterians, Church of Christ, and Catholics. I don't remember any non-denominational congregations in those days. All the churches were physically close to each other, but I do not recall one day of disagreements among the Christian community. I believe that my dad had a part in that because wherever we lived he created or was active in the local Christian alliance.

Many people believe that preachers' kids are the worst.
I think that my sisters and I were the exceptions to that
thought. I believe that we behaved relatively well – especially
for a preacher's kids. I was always proud that my dad
dedicated his life to preaching the gospel.

My first memory was as a two-year-old in Pine Bluff, Arkansas.
I had pneumonia and was lying in an oxygen tent. I can still
see my sisters looking at me in that tent. By that point in time,
I think they liked me. They had reconciled that I was in the
family to stay.

From then my memory skips until when I was five years old.
I did not attend kindergarten and began my first grade of
school in McNeil, Arkansas. I was the youngest in my class.
Because of my October birthday, I was always among the
youngest in every grade through school.

My first-grade classroom had four grades that were taught in
the same room. The first and second grades were on one side
of the room and the third and fourth grades were on another
side. It is hard to imagine now, but my teacher taught both
the first and second grades. And, her husband taught the
third and fourth grades. There were probably eight or so kids
in each grade, so my teacher split her time between the two
classes.

Laurel, Mississippi

When I was eight years old, we moved to
Laurel, Mississippi. I loved Laurel, as did
all of our family. I completed the fourth-
through-seventh grades there.

That's where my love of sports began and
I was a big fan of the Laurel High Golden

Tornados. I played baseball, football, basketball, golf … whatever sport was in season at the time.

Back in those days, Little League baseball was played by kids between the ages of nine and twelve years old. As a nine-year-old, I played catcher for the Braves. I was a really good catcher and could throw anyone out who was trying to steal. They nicknamed me Yogi, which stuck with me until we moved away from Laurel. My catching was good, but my batting was terrible. As a nine-year-old, I struck out every time I batted. Every time. I didn't even hit a foul ball.

When the next season rolled around, I was inserted into the ninth hitting position, just like I had anchored the previous year. When it was my first turn to bat in the new season, I smashed a pitch over the centerfield fence. I didn't know what to do. I jogged around the bases shaking hands with every opposing player who was anywhere close to where I was running. That was a sweet feeling. My Little League career wound up to be a good one. I became an all-star for three seasons and led the league in hitting as a twelve-year-old. I still have the certificate recognizing my league-leading batting average of .670.

I enjoyed all sports. I was quarterback on the Gardner Elementary football team and came in second in the punt, pass, and kick contest as a sixth-grader. In basketball, I played on the Jones Junior High eighth-grade team while I was in the seventh grade. It would not be long though before everyone caught and passed me in athletic ability.

Laurel was also the site of my inauguration into public speaking. While I was in the seventh grade, my dad encouraged me to enter the Optimist Club oratory contest, so I did. The topic was "Optimism … Youth's Greatest Asset." The contest featured young men from the seventh to ninth grade speaking in front of an audience of 30 or so Optimist Club members. I was the youngest in the competition. I am not sure how many guys beat me in the contest, but I know that I didn't win. However, that contest taught me some important lessons.

First, I was scared to death and had to face that fear head on. Second, I had to learn how to logically prepare a message and connect with the audience. My dad was a big help in that area. Third, I learned that even though I didn't win, the experience was incredibly valuable. Little did I know that one five-minute talk would have such a positive influence on my life. I enjoyed being on stage and sharing a message that I believed. That has not changed in all these years.

Another interesting experience while living in Laurel was that in my sixth-grade Mississippi history class, I had to memorize the counties of Mississippi in alphabetical order. For whatever reason, that memory stuck even to this day … Adams, Alcorn, Amite, Attala, Benton, Bolivar …. You would be surprised how much entertainment that knowledge has provided me. For instance, while working at Xerox as sales planning manager in Memphis, I was responsible for re-aligning sales territories. I was working alongside a lady named Gloria O'Neill. We were in our third day of manipulating the territories in Mississippi when I told Gloria, "I am so tired of looking at all these maps, I bet I could tell you every county in the state of Mississippi." Naturally she called my bluff. I began rattling off every county in alphabetical order. Her eyes popped open. She could not believe that I had memorized those counties while working on that project. I never told her anything different.

Moving from Laurel was sad for our family. Sherry graduated from high school there and Evelyn still has lifelong friends from Laurel. The most important event for me while in Laurel was that as a nine-year-old young boy, I gave my life to Christ. I was baptized by my dad on the first Sunday night in February 1963 at Parkview Baptist Church. My Christian journey began right then, and I am still on my journey.

I will always have fond memories of Laurel.

Mount Pleasant, Texas

Mount Pleasant, Texas, was our next home. My dad pastored Jefferson Avenue Baptist Church. Many of my best days as a kid happened in Mount Pleasant, a town of about 30,000 people in East Texas. We lived there while I was in the eighth and ninth grades.

During the eighth and ninth grade in Mount Pleasant, I was quarterback for the Tigers and played basketball, baseball, and ran track. In track, I ran the second leg of the mile relay team that set a ninth-grade record in the state of Oklahoma. I never had much stamina and could not run long distances. Every single practice I would throw up after running 440 yards. For whatever reason, I could not pace myself and would run full speed all the way.

I learned years later that my business career would be much the same … go as hard as I could and then throw up and come back the next day.

It was also in Mount Pleasant that I realized the pain of death and the reality of sudden loss. I had experienced my grandparents' passing, but that was a natural occurrence. I assumed that older people were supposed to die, but not younger people. Due to two events, it became real that we all have a short window of life, which could be closed at any time. While in Mount Pleasant, I lost two classmates in an automobile accident and Evelyn lost one of her best friends in a separate accident. Those were dark days. The young people in our school tried to reconcile how tragedy could happen to good people who did not deserve death. I still have difficulty reconciling that question. I have seen the mystery of prayers answered with a miracle, but some things happen to us that I will never fully understand.

Partially due to those events, I thought I wanted to be a mortician to help families through their tragedy. While that career path vanished somewhere along the way, I believe that my current mission in life of encouraging people may have originated through those tragedies.

We lived in Mount Pleasant for only two years. However, those years were definitely among my best. I have maintained friendships from there, including Alford Flanagan, who is the only person who was in my wedding and I was in his. He and I double-dated on our first dates with Kathy Pate and Suzy Grumbles. Suzy was my date, and I still think she was the best-looking girl in Mount Pleasant at the time.

Baker, Louisiana

After resigning from our church in Mount Pleasant, my dad accepted the pastoral call to a church in Baker, Louisiana, a suburb of Baton Rouge. By then, both of my sisters were in college and I was the only kid living at home. Baker was not a good fit for my dad or anyone in my family. I do not know the inner workings of the church there, but my memory is that none of our family were happy. We only lived in Baker for six months.

Texarkana, Arkansas

Our next move was to Texarkana, Arkansas, where Dad was the pastor of Central Baptist Church. I was happy to move back into the more familiar surroundings of Arkansas and to be only 60 miles from Mount Pleasant. Our home in Texarkana – like all the other homes that we lived in – was modest, but when you walked through the front door, you knew it was a welcome and safe harbor.

Texarkana is a name combining the states of Texas, Arkansas, and Louisiana. It is divided down the middle with Texas to the west and Arkansas to the east. Louisiana is about 30 miles south. Even though Texarkana was connected by a state line that split the post office in half – it is the only federal office building to straddle a state line – everyone was either Texan or Arkansan. The Texarkana high schools were the Texas High Tigers and the Arkansas High Razorbacks. The rivalry was fierce. At Arkansas High, every day when I walked in the door, I was greeted by a large neon sign that said BEAT TEXAS.

My high school years were the beginning of my love for Razorbacks and despising the University of Texas. I still do not like anything orange.

My junior year at Arkansas High was the first year of school integration. Booker T. Washington High School juniors and seniors suddenly became students at Arkansas High. It was a challenge for everyone. The integrating students did not feel like they belonged and the white students were not happy, either. It was a time when we all had to figure out how to accept the new reality of our lives. Everyone had to learn how to get along. The blacks had lived quietly and peacefully "across the tracks." The whites had lived quietly and peacefully in their own world. Now, the worlds were being thrown together.

When the Booker T. Washington students entered Arkansas High School, they were expected to exit from their traditions and embrace their new school's traditions. Their mascot had been the Mighty Lions for almost 50 years, but now they were supposed to be Razorbacks. They had their own school songs; now they were supposed to sing our school songs. They were expected to blend into our school without bringing their heritage with them.

Looking back, it is obvious that was not fair or right.

Both football teams had players who had starred on their respective team. Now they were suddenly competing to be a starter on the new, combined team. Many of the white players were threatened by the influx of new talent. Nevertheless, when football practice began, the white and black players worked together relatively well. Everyone on our team wanted to win and worked hard to make that happen.

However, other students in our school did not blend in with a common goal as well as the football players did. There was tension in the classrooms, starting with the first day of school.

Arkansas High had rich traditions that the new students from Booker T. Washington were expected to adapt to. One of the traditions was our fight song, "Dixie," which had been played at Arkansas High games for decades. The black students were offended by the words of the song, words that the white students could not comprehend as being so offensive. Regardless, the new students petitioned our band leaders to abandon "Dixie" as our fight song. The band leaders responded that it was too late to abandon the song for that year since football season was already in progress.

That decision was unacceptable to the black students. They planned to riot if our band continued to play "Dixie."

Because of the influx of new students, our school pep rally had to be relocated from the gym, where we had traditionally held them, to the football stadium. On October 10, our opponent that Friday night was the Hot Springs Trojans, one of our rivals. The morning of the game, our students gathered in the football stadium for a pep rally. The morning was cool and crisp.

There was a buzz around campus that if the band played "Dixie," something was going to happen.

The entire student body filed into the stadium. The band was on the south end of the stands, players were on the field, and the remainder of the students were in the stands right in front of the team. We, the team, had a perfect view from the field and saw that something was strange. All of the black students were at the very top of the stadium – primarily on the top two rows. When the band played the first chord of "Dixie," all hell broke loose. The black students rained down from the top of the stadium, pushing and shoving the rest of the students all the way through the chain-link fence that separated the fans from the players. People were flying all over the place. Blood was covering some of the students' clothing.

It was a frightening moment.

From our seats on the field, our team could see the riot unfold. Our coaches responded quickly and told us to *get into the field house NOW*. All of our players, black and white, went directly inside the field house where we remained sequestered. We did not know what was happening outside.

Within 30 minutes, our coaches said we were going to
Hot Springs right then, so we loaded up the buses. When
we reached Hot Springs, about a couple of hours from
Texarkana, they checked us into a hotel. There we were,
blacks and whites together in a hotel, before we were to play
Hot Springs that evening. We were having a good time.

Back at the school, things were not good. The riot had been
severe. Several people were hurt and sent to the hospital,
although no one was severely injured. The school was closed
for the remainder of the day.

Meanwhile, my parents were aware of the riot and were
concerned for my safety. They knew I was safe with the team
in Hot Springs but were worried about me driving home
when we returned from the game. My mom went to the
school and parked my 1964 Ford Falcon in a direction so
that when I left the school, I would be headed directly toward
our house. She wanted me to come straight home when we
returned around midnight.

We played the game and won 7-0. We played as a team and
were oblivious to the happenings back in Texarkana. Upon
our return, a couple of my black teammates needed a ride
home. I volunteered to take them. We got into my car, and I
immediately made a U-turn, driving my Falcon to the "other
side of the tracks." I let my teammates off at their homes and
returned safely to my home. It freaked my mom out that I
had put myself in "danger." I did not see it that way. I was just
giving my teammates a lift home.

After the riots, we had policemen at every entrance and
stairway in our school for the remainder of the school year.
Other than a few normal high-school scuffles, we did not

experience any more racial issues at Arkansas High. To my knowledge, our band did not play "Dixie" one more time … which was okay with me and the rest of our team.

I had a good, not great, athletic career at Arkansas High. One of the major highlights of my Razorback career was playing the best football game of my career against Texas High my junior year. I had 13 tackles in that game.

Another highlight was that I was the first player to bat for our newly formed Razorback baseball team. Our team was good. We rolled over most of our competition. In mid-season, the defending Arkansas state champs and No. 1 team in the state – Little Rock Catholic – came to Texarkana for a doubleheader. We won both games and propelled ourselves to No. 1 in the state. In the state tournament, we cruised until the finals where the big, bad Little Rock Catholic team was our opponent again. This time, when everything was on the line, they whipped us like a bunch of yard dogs. Later, several of those guys became friends of mine at the University of Arkansas.

On the academic side, I was also good, not great. I was much more interested in sports and my girlfriend, Camille, than studying.

My grades were okay, but I never put a lot of emphasis on grades. However, one teacher, Mrs. Beck, had a profound impact on me. Mrs. Beck taught junior English composition. I enjoyed writing, but excelling in her class was not at the top of my priority list. I would turn in each assignment for her class on time, but she would always return it. Before handing the paper back to me, she would tell me, "You can do better than this." That process may have gone on two or three times before she would finally accept my paper. She saw more potential in me than I could see in myself. I never forgot her lesson. I am thankful that she would not accept less than my best. I have used those same words, "You can do better than this," on each of my children and on many people whom I have coached through the years.

My first year out of high school, I attended Texarkana Junior College. I lived at home and worked at Griffin's Furniture and Lighting to save money so I could go off to college. Working was a good experience for me as I was able to attend a General Electric sales school in Shreveport, which whetted my appetite for professional selling.

During that time, our nation had a lottery to determine who would be drafted to serve in the military. Each day of the year was printed on Ping-Pong-like balls. The government would randomly draw the balls and you were assigned a number from 1 to 365, based on your birthday. That number determined if you would be drafted into the military. The U.S. participation in the Vietnam War was winding down, but we were still sending troops there to fight. When it was time for the lottery, the local radio stations would air the results as the balls were drawn. I remember sitting around waiting to hear my number. It did not take long. October 4 was lottery number 79.

In past years, everyone with a number less than 150 had been drafted, although some received an education or religious exemption. I thought for sure that, instead of attending Arkansas or some other university of my choice, I would be going to rice – the rice fields of Vietnam that is. However, the draft was abolished that year.

The University of Arkansas

After Texarkana Junior College, I attended the University of Arkansas in Fayetteville, about 250 miles north of Texarkana. Fayetteville was an active college town for the 10,000 students enrolled at the university. I chose marketing as my major and finance as my minor.

I enjoyed my time in college, but one class that was a major challenge for me was Computers 101. It may be hard to believe, but we only had one computer on the business campus – only one. My college days were before Bill Gates and Steve Jobs created friendly, easy-to-use, intuitive software. We had to code our input using FORTRAN or COBOL. If you don't know what that is, I can't explain it to you. I would stand in line with my computer cards and wait my turn for the one computer, which was located in a large room where the temperature was about 40 degrees at all times. The computer would spit out rolls of paper that had green and white sections on it and I would then find out if my project was programmed correctly or not. If there was an error, I had to go to the back of the line and start all over.

In other business classes, I had more success. In Business Communications Writing, my instructor was a graduate assistant. The syllabus for that class was pretty easy for me and I coasted along. The grad assistant pulled me aside and told me almost the same words that Mrs. Beck had told me a few years before. "You will probably get an 'A' in this class, but you are not giving it your best shot. You have the talent to write better than this. Why don't you use it?" That was the second time I heard a similar message that I may have a gift in business communication. I graduated from the University of Arkansas with a degree in Marketing in May 1975.

After graduation, many of the university marketing students went to work at a relatively new and growing retail company located just 20 miles north in Bentonville, Arkansas. Walmart was just beginning to expand outside of rural Arkansas. I briefly considered applying at Walmart. However, during my senior year, Griffin's Furniture and Lighting – where I had worked during junior college – burned to the ground. Dale Griffin, the owner, asked if I would come back to Texarkana and help him open his new, rebuilt store. I said that I would.

Upon graduation, I moved back to Texarkana. I worked hard to try to make my experience there different now that I was a full-time employee rather than just a part-timer. I found that difficult. I discovered that I had much more responsibility but not that much more maturity. Several of my high school friends never left Texarkana and were basically in the same space they were in high school. When I was around them, I found myself returning to my high school days' behavior as well.

We re-opened Griffin's Furniture and Lighting in the early fall of 1975. Shortly afterward, I filled up my 1973 Oldsmobile Cutlass Supreme, which I had bought new for $4,200, with every possession I had and took off for Houston to begin my adult life and business career.

Your Grace of New Experiences Applied

Moving around was challenging for me. If I had been able to vote on whether to move or stay, I would have probably voted against every move. I would have preferred to develop deeper roots and not leave friends instead of having to find new ones. The fact is that I did not have a vote and every move forced me to learn to change, adapt, and see things from a different perspective.

If you are like most, you probably resist significant changes, too. I am not suggesting that you move your family to a new city, but maybe you could see things from a little different perspective right where you are.

What if you looked at some of the people around you like Mrs. Beck looked at me? She provided me a perspective that I did not see in myself. What if you became an encourager for someone who was in a new and awkward environment? What if you took the time to genuinely understand why people do things differently than you?

You will see at least a few people today whom you can and should change your perspective about. They may need to be given another chance to do things better. They may need confidence. They may need a positive role model.

Look around. There may be a situation that is not fair or right and you can make it better. Or, maybe it is time to move away from the influence of some stagnant friends who are not interested in accepting responsibility for their growth.

Complacency is the root of mediocrity. Maybe it is time to stretch yourself into some new experiences that will help you become the person you want to become.

three

Grace of Work

First Job – Xerox in Houston, Texas

I wanted to work for Xerox or IBM.
Xerox offered and IBM turned me down.

I was 22 years old when I pulled into the dynamic city of
Houston, Texas, ready to conquer the world. In 1975,
Houston was a bustling town of about two million people.
When I arrived, I knew three out of the two million – my Aunt
Ruby, Uncle Charles, and cousin Rita. Ruby had offered for
me to stay in their home while I searched for a job.

Finding a job was not something I thought would be difficult
in a town like Houston, but it was. At that time, the best
companies for training and developing young college
graduates were IBM and Xerox. I really wanted to work at
the top of the class. I took a pre-employment personality-
and-aptitude test at both of those companies. I did not hear
anything back for several weeks.

I applied at several other organizations and, after about
a month, I felt that I had worn out my welcome at Aunt
Ruby's home. I loaded up my car and took off for Dallas

to go through the same job application routines that I had completed in Houston. My sister Sherry and brother-in-law Tommy allowed me to stay at their home during my job search. I went to several companies and applied for openings they had in Dallas. I received an offer from the Federal Reserve Bank, but auditing banks didn't exactly float my boat.

Finally, I received a call from Xerox in Houston. I immediately drove from Dallas to Houston for the interview. The next day I received the job offer that I was hoping for. My salary would be $750 a month plus commissions. My goal was to make $12,000 a year, and this job would allow me to maybe even make a little more. To put things in perspective, the median income at that time was $12,686, and I had a chance to eclipse that my first year out of college. I would be a sales representative for Xerox.

By the way, IBM formally turned me down, but I got over that quickly. Life was good.

I am forever grateful to Richard Davenport, the Xerox sales planning manager, who endorsed me, and to Bob Naughton, the branch manager at their downtown Houston office. Bob took a chance on a really, really green but fiery guy when he offered me the job.

After about four weeks of studying our products, it was time to go to Xerox's corporate training facility in Leesburg, Virginia. When I boarded the plane in Houston to fly to Washington, D.C., it was the first time that I had ever been on a commercial aircraft. My only previous flight was in a small Cessna-type plane a few years before. Upon arrival at Washington National and after retrieving my luggage, there was a 12-seat van waiting to take me and several others about 30 miles to the training facility.

The Xerox facility in Leesburg was brand new and cutting-edge. It was incredible. The training schedule was three intense weeks in Leesburg, return home for two weeks, and then return to Leesburg for three more weeks. The first day of class, each new hire took a test. If you failed the test, you were sent home. It was stressful, and there were a few of my classmates whom I never saw again after that day.

Leesburg was a dramatic learning experience for me in several ways. First, the talent surrounding me was intimidating. It appeared to me that every person was smarter and more experienced in all areas of life than I was. I worked hard, real hard, to keep up with my classmates when it came to product knowledge and processes. However, when it came to sales training, that was right up my alley and I was able to excel a little more.

At that time, Xerox taught a sales process called PSS – Professional Selling Skills. It was a strictly defined method of asking specific questions so that you could understand the customer's business and provide appropriate solutions. I loved it. The game of selling intrigued me and I was zealous about becoming the best salesperson at Xerox. It was also the first time that I had been able to practice on videotape and see for myself where I could improve.

My lifelong passion for personal development and improvement began in my first sales training class in Leesburg, Virginia.

Another dramatic learning experience for me in Leesburg happened during my second three-week training period. One of my classmates was Owen Brown, a former star forward and co-captain of the University of Maryland's 1975 championship basketball team. Owen was a charismatic, nice guy who just happened to be a thin, six-foot, eight-inch former basketball star. He was playing in a pickup game in our Leesburg gym. He played for about 30 minutes when all of the sudden he fell over.

Owen was dead before any medical help could arrive. He was 22 years old, the same age I was at that time. He was in great shape but had a rare form of heart disease called hypertrophic cardiomyopathy. The heart is enlarged and the wall between the right and left ventricles is abnormally thick. All of his physicals at Maryland were fine until a stress test before his senior season revealed an irregular heartbeat. After consultation with a cardiologist, who told him that the risk was minor, Owen made the decision to continue playing. He played his senior year and completed his four years of eligibility at Maryland without incident. Then, in a casual pickup game in Leesburg, he died.

Again, just like when I was faced with the sting of death during my ninth-grade year, I struggled with the fairness of life and death and how little control we have over how long we live.

I loved working for Xerox in Houston. I was able to expand my awareness of other people and cultures. It was a dynamic, winning company. I was proud to present my business card that identified me as a sales representative for one of the best companies in the world at that time.

While in Houston, my largest sale was a facility management agreement with Mitchell Energy in The Woodlands, Texas. The agreement was that Xerox would provide the labor, equipment, and supplies for Mitchell's copy center. The Woodlands was an isolated area then and Mitchell was having trouble employing people to run their copying operation. Xerox's facilities management solution was perfect for them. It was the sixth facilities management agreement in the country. I received an upfront bonus of $1,500. That was a big deal. In addition to the bonus, my normal quota was reduced by 25 percent for a year. That may still reign as the "biggest" sale of my career.

Houston was a great city for me. My life began to change and improve spectacularly while I lived there.

Your Grace of Work Applied

One of our greatest gifts is the gift of work. If you don't agree, just ask someone who is not physically or mentally able to work. They would give anything to have your job.

I have experienced all forms of emotions and outcomes during my career:

- Frustration over doing a great job yet not experiencing a great financial outcome
- Sadness in having to say goodbye to an employee or a company
- Pride in working for a world-class organization
- Disappointment in creating a great business plan that didn't work out
- Satisfaction in taking a chance, working hard, and experiencing significant financial gain

What have I learned through all of this? I have learned that the secret to success always includes hard work. By hard work, I mean getting up, getting with it, using my time wisely, and making the most of the day.

It also means setting goals and creating a plan to reach that goal. I did not have the luxury to coast. I had to get up early, follow my plan, and then do it again the next day.

Work is your conduit to choices. It allows you to choose how to spend your time, resources, relationships, where you live, and what you provide your family. I have found that the people who enjoy work the most are those who are really good at their job. If you are not the best yet, find out who the best is and spend time with them. Pick their brain and see if they are doing something a little different that you could do to become better.

Many people consider work a burden instead of a gift, and they work just to get by. I hope that you will make the decision to be one of the few-and-far-between people who give everything you have while at work. Then, you will have the freedom to make better choices in other areas of your life. In my experience, the best employees are those who are balanced in their work and personal life and work toward a purpose.

There is no reason to work just to get tired.

Even if you love your work, if you are like most, you will occasionally lose your spirit. Unexpected things happening in your life will quench your inner fire. It may be barely a flicker. When that happens, don't try to rekindle the fire by yourself. Find a mentor, friend, or someone who has the wisdom to help you fan the small flicker and allow it to flame again.

Perhaps you are at the age and stage that you can be the wise counsel for someone whose flame is almost out. If so, I hope that you will choose to be the person who helps someone fan their small flicker. Don't be surprised that when you help fuel someone's flickering flame, it will ignite your fire as well.

four

Grace of Love

Engaged, Married, and Baby

Every love story is delightful, but this is my favorite.

My first apartment in Houston was in Napoleon Square – a huge complex whose residents were young adults. It had a restaurant and bar, so it was a magnet for young people like me.

I quickly discovered that even though there were a lot of people around me, the big city was quite a lonely place.

All of my life had been centered around church activities. I had "wandered" for a little while as a junior in college but had returned to my spiritual foundation by my senior year. Now things were different. I was in foreign territory. I did not have anyone to go to church with me and I had to force myself to get up and go on my own. The first, and only, church I visited was First Baptist, Houston. It was a downtown church and the pastor was John Bisagno, a dynamic minister. First Baptist had a large and active young adult ministry.

The first time I attended Bible study there, I sat beside a beautiful, young, five-foot, three-inch brunette who was wearing a white dress. We made eye contact and introduced ourselves to each other. Her name was Karen Pearce. That brief introduction was the last time I saw or spoke to her for a while. She sang in the choir, and the choir members left Bible study a few minutes before it ended to change into their choir robes and get ready for the church service. Consequently, I was not able to spark a conversation with her in the time between Bible study and church. I took close notice of her singing in the choir and wondered what her story was.

Then, I left town to attend my second round of sales training in Leesburg for three weeks. When I finally returned to Houston and attended First Baptist again, I sat close to her in Bible study. But, again I was not able to strike up a conversation before she left with the other choir members.

The following weekend, the young adults had a retreat at Waterwood, a resort north of Houston. There was a golf outing on that Saturday morning, so I signed up to go and play golf and attend the retreat.

The retreat began at two o'clock. I finished playing golf, changed clothes, and made it to the first session of the retreat just in time. Lo and behold, as I walked in, there sat Karen. I walked over and asked if anyone was sitting next to her. She said that she was holding a spot for one of her friends, but there was plenty of room for all. So, I finally had a chance to talk to her.

I broke the ice by asking her what she did for a living and found out that she was a schoolteacher in Texas City, about 20 miles southeast of Houston. She graduated from Bellaire High School in the Houston area and from Stephen F. Austin University in Nacogdoches, Texas. We began filling in the blanks about each other during each break of that weekend retreat. When the retreat was over, I asked her to save me a spot in our Bible study class on Sunday.

When I walked into the Bible study class the next day, I was happy to see that there was an empty chair next to her waiting for me.

A group at the retreat planned to go out to eat after church that Sunday night. I asked Karen if she wanted to ride with me. She said "yes," but she allowed herself an "out" by saying that she had to get home early and prepare for her school day on Monday. So, we went to Luther's, a popular barbecue restaurant in Houston. We were there with about 30 other people … and we were the last to leave.

That was the beginning of a special relationship.

One of my personal traits is that I am decisive. When I see something that I am interested in pursuing – in business or in life – I get moving pretty fast. My courtship with Karen was no different.

Our first date was a Xerox employee dinner. She had a knack of being able to get along with about anyone and she fit right in with my fellow workers and spouses. I was liking what I saw. We began seeing each other almost every day.

In early June of 1976, I was a groomsman in a wedding in Fayetteville, Arkansas. I asked her if she would like to go with me on the 12-hour trip. We would cut the trip in half by staying at my parents' home in Texarkana. So, not only was she going to be with me in a car for four days and sit by herself at a wedding of someone she didn't know, she was also going to meet my parents. She took all of that in stride and we took off for Fayetteville.

That trip was really good. She met some of my friends, but most importantly she met my mom and dad. Dad, being a pastor, knew a lot about people as he had seen it all in his day. I was interested to hear what his opinion of this girl from Houston would be.

I called him to get his take when I returned to Houston. He was impressed with her and so was my mom. I told him that I might marry her and asked him what he thought about that since I had only known her a short while. He listened to me for several minutes and then said, "It doesn't matter how long you know someone. I have counseled many couples who knew each other all their lives and their marriages didn't last. What matters is how well you know them. What are their values? How do they respond when things do not go well? How do they get along with their family? Who are their friends? What is their spiritual commitment?" I knew that Karen would pass each of those tests with flying colors.

Soon after that conversation with my dad, I wanted her to meet the rest of my family. So we took another weekend trip up to the Dallas area where both of my sisters lived. We had dinner at Sherry's house, and I remember how Sherry and Evelyn sat on each side of Karen on the sofa. Immediately she fit in with my sisters like she was one of them. While they were engaged in a conversation, it was as though I was the outsider.

I was convinced that she was the person I wanted to spend the rest of my life with.

One evening while we were sitting in my new apartment in Northwest Houston, I asked her what she thought about the possibility of getting married. She was shocked at first to hear that question, but we quickly got into a serious conversation about what our future would look like together. We both liked what we saw. We decided to pray about it and sit on the decision for a little while.

In my world, a little while is a very little while. The following Saturday, I took Karen to Corrigan's Jewelers where a friend of ours worked. We started looking at wedding rings and we agreed on the perfect ring for her. Our friend said that it would be two weeks before the ring would be sized and ready. So, I had a couple of weeks to figure out the best way to formally ask the love of my life to marry me.

Engaged

Vargo's was a fine, romantic restaurant in Houston. Behind the restaurant, they had a beautiful garden that was hidden just a short way from the bright lights of Houston. It was so isolated that you would think that it was in the middle of the woods. The walking path meandered around some incredible flowers and there were a couple of park benches situated along that beautiful setting. I thought that would be the perfect place for me to ask her to marry me. So, I called for reservations for two for Saturday evening, July 24, 1976. Everything was set. I would pick up the ring on Friday and we would go to Vargo's Saturday evening.

We were both looking forward to that dinner.

I drove to Corrigan's in downtown Houston and picked up the ring as scheduled that Friday afternoon. I called Karen and told her that the ring had not arrived and it would be the following week before it would be in. I suggested that we go ahead with our plan to eat at Vargo's and we could create a new plan for the next weekend. She was disappointed, but we agreed that another week was not going to make a big difference in the scope of things.

Finally, Saturday arrived. We both dressed up to go to Vargo's, even though she did not think that night would be as special as we had planned. The meal was spectacular. While we were enjoying our dinner, Karen made the comment that "This would be a perfect evening if the jeweler had gotten our ring to us on time." I did not say anything. For years after that, though, she heard from me, "This would be a perfect evening if …." That statement became a staple of laughter in our marriage.

The setting was fabulous. Even though I had spent several days' wages on the dinner, in Karen's mind the guy at the jewelry store had "ruined" it. I asked her if she wanted to walk through the garden anyway. Thankfully she said sure. As we walked through the garden, we came to one of the park benches. I said, "It is a beautiful evening, let's sit here a while and enjoy it." So we did. After a minute or so, I got on my knee, pulled the ring from my jacket pocket and formally proposed right there … just like we had planned. The great surprise, after the disappointment, made the evening even better.

From that day forward we made it a point to search for our great surprise after we faced a disappointment. And, I had a pretty good story to tell for the rest of our lives.

Once engaged, we began talking about the right date to marry. Our pastor led us through a pretty intense four-week premarital counseling session. Our outlook on faith, money, friends, children, and other decisions that we would make as a couple was perfectly aligned.

At first we agreed on a January wedding. Then, we decided a December wedding would be better. Then, with my pushing, we decided to move it up to around Thanksgiving.

November 20, 1976, the weekend before Thanksgiving, would be our day.

One of the discoveries Karen made during our brief courtship was my love of the Arkansas Razorbacks. The first game we attended together was at Rice University. We were sitting among all of the Razorback fans dressed in red and it was time to call the Hogs, a tradition of Razorback sports. She did not know what was going on and was innocently sitting and waiting for the game to begin. I told her to get off her butt and call the hogs! That was the last time I told her that. I learned my lesson and, fortunately, we spent a significant portion of our life cheering on the Razorbacks.

Married

Finally, our wedding day arrived. November 20 was a cold, rainy day in Houston. We were married in the afternoon; I think around 5 p.m. The wedding was in the vast sanctuary of First Baptist, Houston. There were about 200 people at  the wedding, and Pastor John Bisagno and my dad were the officiates. My dad was also my best man. It was a good day.

Back then, Baptist weddings were simpler because the reception was in the fellowship hall of the church. By seven that evening, the wedding and celebration were over.

Everyone threw rice on us as we loaded up in Karen's green Chevy Malibu and headed toward New Orleans for our honeymoon.

That was the first day of a grand 36 years of marriage.

We spent our first night together in a honeymoon suite in Beaumont, Texas. We were trying to be discreet about being newlyweds, but when we checked into the hotel, the young man who was helping with our luggage said in a voice loud enough for everyone in the lobby to hear, "*Whoo. The Honeymoon Suite. You just get married?*" So much for being discreet. We smiled as we received an ovation in the lobby.

When we arrived in New Orleans, we checked into the Royal Bourbon Hotel in the French Quarter without any fanfare. It was cold and damp, but that did not prevent us from taking in all of the tourist attractions. We took a horse-and-buggy ride, rode the street car, went to the race track, and ate until we couldn't eat any more.

Karen loved to laugh. We laughed together our entire marriage. One of our first laughs together as a married couple was on the second night of our honeymoon. We were at Pat O'Brien's, a popular club in the French Quarter. Karen took a liking to the famous Pat O'Brien's Hurricane – I told her it was just like a strawberry slush. She enjoyed her second Hurricane even more than her first. We were in the room where a man was "playing" music with his fingers and coins on a tray. The place was packed. We were sitting around a table with five or six total strangers and Karen began rubbing my leg. After a few minutes, she looked down and it was not *my* leg she was rubbing. It was a random college professor from Northeast Louisiana University. The guy said it was the biggest thrill he had while in New Orleans. He also told us that he was relieved to discover that it was not me doing the rubbing.

We returned to Houston just in time to enjoy Thanksgiving dinner with Karen's family.

Our first apartment together was in the Maple Ridge Apartments, just a short bicycle ride away from her parents. The apartment was about 700 square feet, but it was big enough for us.

Times were good. We both had jobs that we enjoyed. We were very active in our church.

In April 1978, around Karen's birthday on the 10th, things even got a lot better. We had a positive result from a pregnancy test. We checked again; positive again. The next day her doctor confirmed that we had a baby on the way.

Moved

In June, a transfer opportunity with Xerox in Fayetteville, Arkansas, came open. That was a dream for me to go back to my college town. Karen probably wasn't that thrilled, but she was supportive in making that move. As a grandparent now, I can only imagine how disappointed Karen's mom and dad were when we broke the news that we were moving to Arkansas and taking their first grandbaby with us. However, they never said anything about their disappointment … at least to me.

My mom and dad came to Houston to help with our move. We loaded up a Hertz truck for our 500-mile move north to Fayetteville. We moved into a small apartment while we searched for the perfect home for us and our baby. It did not take long until we found our ideal house at 1873 Seminole Ct. We purchased it for $45,000. That may not sound like much money, but it was a lot of money at the time. I was not sure how we were going to make the payments, but we did.

The move to Fayetteville did not start off as a great career move. My sales manager worked out of Little Rock, which was about three hours away. For whatever reason, he did not like me … or anyone else for that matter. He was miserable to work for, although he appeared to be a decent guy one-on-one. Regardless, work life was not a piece of cake with him. The entire time he was in Little Rock, he wanted to be back in Fort Worth where he had been a good sales rep before he was promoted to become a bad manager in Little Rock.

Karen kept encouraging me to hang in there; he was temporary. Sure enough, he was. He got a job with Acme Brick in Fort Worth. He was able to go back home. There was no going-away party for him, at least that he was invited to. Everyone who worked for him wondered if his job was going to be selling bricks or throwing them.

One of the best things about our new house was the neighbors who lived around us. We soon became lifelong friends with Fred and Beverly Treffinger and Milo and Charlotte Bump. The Bumps were expecting their first baby, as well. Jeremy Bump was born a few weeks before our baby arrived on the scene.

Jennifer Anne Cottrell was born on November 10, 1978, at Washington Regional Hospital in Fayetteville. She was a couple of weeks premature and weighed in at six pounds and seven ounces. We did not know the sex of the child until delivery. We were both thrilled to have a baby girl.

Driving home from the hospital where I had just seen our baby for the first time, I remember having cold chills. I was excited and terrified at the same time. My life had just changed forever.

Stevie Wonder had recently released an album titled *Songs in the Key of Life,* which featured a magnificent song: "Isn't She Lovely." We immediately bought the album and almost wore the vinyl out playing the song. The lyrics perfectly described how we felt:

> *Isn't she lovely?*
> *Isn't she wonderful?*
> *Isn't she precious?*
> *Less than one minute old*
> *I never thought through love we'd be*
> *Making one as lovely as she*
> *But isn't she lovely made from love*
> *I can't believe what God has done through us He's given life to one*
> *But isn't she lovely made from love.*

Regardless of what was happening around us, baby Jennifer made life better. Fred and Beverly felt the same way. They loved Jennifer and would come to our house and hold her every night.

Karen loved Jennifer. She would wrap her arms around Jennifer like Saran Wrap and snuggle her. Her smile was ear-to-ear.

She had many talents, but she was born to be a mom.

Your Grace of Love Applied

I really enjoyed writing this chapter. It has love, surprise, laughter, disappointment, and the miracle of our first child, all in these few pages.

It has also been clear, as I look back, that not all of my choices were easy. One of the truths that I learned many years ago is that you will become like the people you surround yourself with. That can be a blessing or a curse.

During my early days in Houston, I didn't know anyone. I had to consciously make a decision of who I wanted to hang around. There were plenty of opportunities in the apartment complex where I lived. But, the more I looked around, the more obvious it became to me that I did not want to live like most of them were living.

The most comfortable and safe place for me had always been in the church. It was not much fun to go there alone, but it was a secure place for me. It also was where I found the person who would be a blessing for me to spend the rest of my life.

If you have children, one of your greatest fears is that someone whose values are different from yours will influence your child in a negative way. You realize that your child may make a life-changing decision influenced by a person you may have never met.

As adults, we are subject to many more things that influence our behaviors. We have access to more information, opinions, and fake news than ever before. If you spend your time dwelling on one "channel" of information, that is who you will become.

I hope you will take this lesson seriously: You will emulate the people and information that you surround yourself with. If you look around, you will not have to search far to find evidence of curses and blessings.

five

Grace of Faith

Outside My Comfort Zone – Move to Memphis

I believe that God answers prayer in one of four ways:
slow, grow, no, or go. This time I was convinced,
without a doubt, it was a GO.

My business career had settled down after my former sales
manager moved back to Fort Worth. My new sales manager
was a great guy named Fred Collins. Fred and I got along well
and we are still friends to this day. One time he sent his boss,
Tony Van Roekel, to makes sales calls with me in Fayetteville.
Tony was a charismatic 40-something guy and we had a
couple of good sales days together. I did not know it at the
time, but when he returned from that trip, he told Fred, "We
have to get that guy out of the boonies and into a city where
he can make a bigger difference."

I was perfectly content as a sales rep in Fayetteville. There
was no reason for me to go anywhere in a lateral move. But, I
had completed a Xerox pre-manager course in Dallas and was
preparing to become a manager.

Then, the old axiom that *success happens when opportunity meets preparation* came alive for me.

November 18, 1980, was just another day making sales calls until I received an unexpected telephone call. On the other end of the phone was Fred Collins, who shared the news: "Xerox is reorganizing, and some new opportunities are coming up. Can you meet me in Memphis tomorrow?" That sounded like it could be the opportunity that I had been preparing for, so I took off for Memphis.

Xerox was splitting its organization into two divisions: the Business Product Division (BPD) and the Information System Division (ISD). This was a big deal and it created enormous career opportunities. BPD was the new division, which would be focusing on addressing the aggressive, new, foreign competition in the small copier market. BPD would sell to smaller organizations. ISD would sell to the larger organizations.

Fortunately for me and everyone else in our division, Tony Van Roekel would be the Memphis branch manager of BPD. One of the jobs created in the reorganization was a sales planning manager whose job would be to hire and train new sales representatives. The next day, Tony offered me the sales planning manager position. I was barely 26 years old and became one of the youngest – possibly *the* youngest – managers working for Xerox.

We loved Fayetteville, but this career opportunity was too good to pass up. Memphis would not have been on our *Top Places to Live* list, but it became a wonderful place for our family. Xerox bought our Fayetteville home and, after a brief search, we found our new home at 2905 Elmridge Cove in Germantown, Tennessee. The house was substantially larger than our house in Fayetteville. We paid $90,000. Again, I was not completely sure how we could afford that house payment.

I believe that I have had three special times in my career when I knew I was the right person in the right job at the right time. The sales planning manager job at Xerox was my first of those times. I was Tony's righthand man and he and I worked together wonderfully. My job was to interview and hire sales representatives, primarily from college campuses. Being on the other side of the interview desk was a fun time for me. I remembered Richard Davenport in that role and the impact that he had on me. I wanted to have the same impact on those that I interviewed. I learned the process of how to interview and select the best candidates during my time at Xerox.

My passion for personal development was ignited at Xerox. Another of my responsibilities as sales planning manager was to train the new salespeople and prepare them for their training classes in Leesburg. I loved to teach and learn from each of those new employees.

My first team as sales manager

Around that time, someone gave me a book titled *See You at the Top* by Zig Ziglar. That was the first book I had read that presented a logical plan on how to be successful. The basis of the plan was to become a continuous learner so that you had better information to make more sound decisions. It made sense to me and helped to broaden my horizons and educate me in the sales and personal development arena. I enjoyed teaching the concepts of that book to our sales teams. It was the first time that I had really been on fire to become the very best that I could.

I spent $5 on a library card and began reading every sales, management, and inspirational book that I could find. I had no idea that I would eventually write books and attempt to inspire others the way those books inspired me.

Time for Another Speech

While at work one day, I received a call from a business professor at Memphis State University. He requested a Xerox leader to come and speak to his MBA class about success. I did not think I was qualified for that role, but Tony convinced me that it would be a good learning experience for me. I don't think that he wanted to do it. Regardless, I took it on. It was to be a 30-minute after-dinner speech and would be my first formal speech since my Optimist Club speech as a seventh-grader.

I believed I had developed some decent content based on the books that I had read and my observations from the few years I had worked. But, I did not know how to put it together. I went to the library and checked out a couple of books on how to prepare a presentation. One common denominator revealed in those books was that people relate to stories. To connect with your audience, tell a story.

I decided that my emphasis in the speech was going to be about how the most successful people were not necessarily the smartest, the highest educated, or even the hardest working – although each of those things help. There is no entitlement in the business world based solely on those factors. The most successful people may do a few things extraordinarily well … better than the average person. More importantly, they did a lot of things just a little better, and the payout for being the best was a lot more than just a little. For instance, the person who comes in second selling earns nothing. The winning salesperson does several things just a little better to earn everything. I began searching for a story to express the points that I was trying to make that my audience could relate to.

Our management team had just returned from a trip that we won to the Kentucky Derby. That year, Pleasant Colony won the derby by a slim margin. The difference in the earnings for Pleasant Colony was staggering compared to the other horses that ran the race. I decided that Pleasant Colony's victory would be my story.

Pleasant Colony was not considered to be the best-bred horse in the derby. He was not favored to win based on his previous performances. No one knew if he trained the hardest, but he figured out a way to win the Kentucky Derby that day.

I had my speech typed out and ready to go. I was fired up. When I got up to speak, there was not enough lighting in the room for me to easily refer to my notes. I almost panicked, but I had practiced enough to get my thoughts across without referring to my notes. Just like I had read in the presentation books, something unexpected will probably happen. And, it did. However, I had prepared well enough to make it through the unexpected. The speech went well. I enjoyed the time. It was a terrific learning experience and I was able to attack most people's greatest fear of speaking in public.

Xerox was a terrific company. As the hiring manager, I was able to be very selective in who I hired. We had plenty of impressive candidates on every college campus where I interviewed. I was able to hire a wave of new sales reps because of the reorganization, and those new hires were the foundation of our district. I wanted the very best to represent our company. We were fortunate enough to attract outstanding reps, and Tony was a terrific branch manager. I went along for the ride and received my first major corporate recognition as the BPD Sales Planning Manager of the Year for the entire company.

The following year, I was promoted into a sales manager position. I had a terrific team and we won several awards. Almost everyone on my team made President's Club. I again rode the wave of their success.

The next year, the sales planning manager (SPM) role became a post-sales manager position. The first time I was the SPM, it was a role to prepare you to become a sales manager. For whatever reason, Xerox flipped the grade level and made the sales planning manager a post-sales manager job. I was promoted again to be an SPM.

I had three major promotions in three years.

During that time while we were enjoying our best business success, Karen had a miscarriage. It was devastating. I had never experienced a loss that hurt so deeply. She was "only" nine weeks pregnant, but losing that baby was excruciatingly painful.

Fortunately, Karen was able to get pregnant soon after the miscarriage and, on February 26, 1982, Kimberly Lynne Cottrell was born at Baptist East Hospital in Memphis. She weighed in at a healthy eight pounds and six ounces. It didn't take long for us to find the Stevie Wonder album and crank up "Isn't She Lovely" again.

I knew that my Xerox days were numbered. I had already dodged a move to the home office in Rochester, New York, and had no desire to relocate to our region in St. Louis or our training facility in Leesburg, Virginia. I had risen as far as I could go without moving farther away from both of our families, who were now all living in Texas.

I enjoyed my job tremendously, but being a sales planning manager at Xerox was not a lifelong career stop.

Your Grace of Faith Applied

As you can see, I had several forks in the road during this time in my life. Which road to choose? How do you make that decision? Is there a process? I asked those questions. My conclusion was that before I made any crucial choices, I had to have a crystal-clear understanding of my values – the few important things that were nonnegotiable in my life.

Many people believe that one of the great things about being in your comfort zone is that there is little risk. You know what to expect most of the time. There are few surprises. You are comfortable.

Actually, a forceful enemy to your potential is your comfort zone. If you want to become your very best, somewhere along the way you will have to leave your comfort zone. In addition, you have to have a firm understanding of what you are willing to sacrifice to become uncomfortable.

For me, I was okay leaving my comfort zone in Fayetteville to relocate to Memphis but not okay with moving to Rochester, St. Louis, or Leesburg. Those three "promotions" would have been in conflict with my priority of not moving any farther away from family in Texas.

You may have to make a similar decision. I have seen several people promoted and it destroyed their family. They did not *predetermine* what was most important to them before they accepted a promotion that cost them the most important thing they had.

A wise mentor once told me to never make a quick, emotional decision about money or my career. That is pretty difficult to do. Your ego and pride are the emotions that drive many decisions. Another piece of advice he provided was to try to measure the impact of any major decision five years forward. He said to question if the decision of today would lead me where I wanted to be in five years. That was good advice that I have tried to follow through the years.

Don't you think it would make sense to talk with your family about your ambitions? It would eliminate stress when something comes along that is emotionally enticing but against what you and your family have decided was important.

In my family, I conducted a family board meeting at least once every six months. It was a time to discuss family issues, make vacation plans, or reinforce our family values. Regardless of age, everyone was a member of our board. Those meetings are some of my most pleasant family memories. It may be something that you want to try as well.

six

Grace of Preparation

Federal Express – Right Place, Right Time

If you're offered a seat on a rocket ship,

don't ask what seat! Just get on.

— SHERYL SANDBERG

During the fall of 1982, I received a call from Carl Williams of Federal Express. When I returned the call, Carl said that I had been recommended to him and he would like to meet me. I was not sure what he might be interested in, but I met him at his office, which was at the corner of Democrat and Republican (no kidding).

The dynamic company, headquartered less than a mile away from my office at Xerox, was literally changing the way that the world did business.

When Federal Express (changed to FedEx in 1990) began operations in 1973, one of its initial advertisements was *There is a new airline in town and it does not have any passengers.* I remember seeing those ads while I was in college, but I didn't pay much attention to what that new company in Memphis was actually doing. A dedicated overnight package delivery concept was new and unproven at the time.

Mark Twain once said, "The man with a new idea is a crank until the idea succeeds," and there were plenty of people calling Fred Smith, the founder of FedEx, a crank in the early '70s. He was a brilliant thought-leader who documented his idea while he was a student at Yale. His professor reportedly gave him a "C" on the paper. His concept was to use a hub-and-spoke system to efficiently move information and products overnight. The FedEx planes would depart their origination city with packages to be delivered all over the United States. They would then all fly to the hub in Memphis and unload the packages they brought, then reload the plane with packages that were destined for their city. The next morning, the packages would be delivered to the recipient. It was definitely outside of the box. Why would you deliver a package from San Francisco to Los Angeles through Memphis? It seemed to defy logic. Today, all of the airlines and package delivery services utilize a hub-and-spoke system for their operations.

FedEx was not an instant success. In fact, on the first night of operation, 14 FedEx planes in 14 cities made their first midnight trip to Memphis. The packages were to be sorted and then reloaded on planes that would take them to their destinations. The entire FedEx team was at the Memphis airport waiting to count the packages and celebrate their success. One by one they unloaded the planes. When all the packages were counted, there were 12 packages total on the 14 planes. That was not a great start.

In its early days, FedEx was on the brink of bankruptcy several times. Smith had supplemented a $4 million inheritance with $91 million in venture capital to get his idea off the ground. There is a well-documented story about Mr. Smith attending a meeting in Chicago in 1976 where he was denied the financial capital that he needed to sustain the company. While at O'Hare Airport, he decided that, instead of going back to Memphis, he would fly to Las Vegas and try to win enough money playing blackjack to make his payroll. He did just that. When he flew back to Memphis, he had enough cash to make payroll for another couple of weeks while he tried to figure out a longer-term solution.

He did.

Fast forward to tonight: While you are sleeping, more than 400,000 FedEx employees will be loading, flying, sorting, re-loading, and flying to their destination more than six million packages. FedEx revenue will exceed $16 billion in 2018.

Electronic Products Division Created

In its early days, FedEx delivered more overnight letters than packages. By 1984, the emerging electronic transmission of information was a threat to the mainstream of FedEx's business.

Until my visit with Carl Williams, I did not know that he was a former Xerox employee and had been working for the fledging new Federal Express for several years. After we shared a few Xerox stories, I signed a nondisclosure agreement. Carl began telling me about a new division that FedEx was creating.

The new electronic product division would be the FedEx answer to the facsimile and electronic transmission race that was diluting overnight letter revenue – which was the most profitable segment of FedEx's business at that time.

FedEx was preparing to create a national sales force to market the new product. Carl was searching for a sales planning manager. I was interested in the project but was not interested in the role he was trying to fill.

Carl then connected me with Chuck Winston, who was the executive vice president of the Electronic Product Division. Chuck and I met a few times and he told me to be patient as he was going to hire the vice president of EPD soon. He hired Bill Razook at the end of 1982. Bill and I began talking, and in early 1983, he offered me the first EPD district manager job, which was headquartered in Memphis.

FedEx was still a relatively small organization. I was excited about this opportunity to work with a new, aggressive organization.

The first time I met Fred Smith, the founder and CEO was in an inauspicious office close to the Memphis airport. The conference table was made of pressed wood – there was no mahogany in sight. It was an exciting place to be. The mission of the Electronic Product Division was to change the way people conducted business, just as the company had changed how business operated a few years before.

I was thrilled to have the opportunity to be on the ground floor of the start-up division.

Xerox had been good to me. I loved the people I worked with and I had hired more than 50 percent of the sales force in the Memphis branch. It was not a tough decision, though. I had been watching FedEx from afar and knew that they were a dynamic organization led by a true Memphis hero, Fred Smith.

Tony Van Roekel had recently accepted a region position in St. Louis. I was not particularly close to the new branch manager, Jim Foreman, so I was not too concerned about handing in my resignation letter to Jim. However, I was very nervous to tell Tony that I was leaving Xerox, an organization that he loved. We both wanted to work together again and Xerox was the only place that would happen.

I decided to tell Tony that I was resigning while we were together at President's Club at The Pointe in Phoenix. We were at the opening-evening cocktail party and I thought that it would be best to tell him as quickly as I could. I pulled him to the side and told him I was leaving Xerox. My voice was cracking. It was like I was telling my father that I was leaving his family. I finally managed to get the words out.

Tony congratulated me and told me that I had been preparing for this opportunity for a long time. He was familiar with FedEx and he thought it could be a great move for me. He gave me his blessing.

I was relieved. I had stressed about that conversation for days. My mentor and friend told me it was okay. The remaining week of President's Club was fantastic.

When I returned to Memphis, I submitted my letter of resignation. I had a wonderful career with Xerox, but it was time for me to move on.

Your Grace of Preparation Applied
Somewhere along the way, you will be offered a chance to do something different. The new opportunity could turn out

to be the perfect job that you have been preparing for all of your life. Or it could be the worst decision that you could make at that junction of your career.

The question is: *How do you know?* I think the best answer was provided by Socrates many years ago when he was quoted as saying:

Know thyself,

combined with my line of today:

Stick with thyself.

The first thing you should know about yourself is the difference between *talent* and *desire.*

Talent is being naturally gifted in a certain area. Desire is something you would like to happen. For instance, I would like to be a professional golfer. However, no matter how hard I work or how much I desire it to happen, I will never be invited to a PGA tournament as a player.

When you know thyself, you will realize that you have talents in areas where you need to spend your energy. Then stick with thyself. You can focus on finding the right place – the right job – that uses your talents and gifts.

Be prepared. You cannot predict when your next opportunity will show up. In the meantime, be the very best at the job that you currently have. That is the best way to have more opportunities come your way.

seven

Grace of Risk

ZapMail – A Gamble Worth Taking

Don't be afraid to take a big step.
You can't cross a chasm in two small jumps.
— DAVID LLOYD GEORGE

By the time I joined FedEx, they were already a huge success story and a well-oiled machine. Fred Smith had correctly identified that a potential threat to the company was the ability to transmit information immediately as opposed to delivering information the next day.

To put his vision in context, there was no Apple, Google, or Amazon in those days. There were no social media, smartphones, cloud computing, texts, tweets, or even voicemail services. The internet was still several years from being invented. The information technology highway was a one-lane dirt road led by companies like Prodigy and CompuServe.

Facsimile machines, with their distinctive, squealing sounds when receiving documents, were expensive. Because of the expense and the requirement of having a dedicated phone line for the machine, fax machines were not in a majority of offices at that time. It did not do you much good if you had a fax machine and the person you needed to send a fax to did not have a machine to receive your information. It would be like having one of the first phones … who would you talk to? In addition, the fax was slowly transmitted through a telephone line and received on rolls of expensive, smelly, chemically treated paper.

However, fax machines were improving and the number of organizations with fax machines was expanding rapidly. At that time, overnight letters were a large percentage of FedEx's business. Even though FedEx was growing rapidly, Fred Smith recognized that his most profitable segment was at risk.

Smith made an aggressive and risky move. His concept was to be the first company to capitalize on the electronic delivery of documents in the same fashion that FedEx was the first to capitalize on the overnight delivery market. The move was an offensive strategy to tap into the surging electronic document market and a defensive strategy for FedEx to continue to receive revenue that would have been diluted from its overnight-delivery-of-letters market.

It was also a way to fill the productivity gap of FedEx employees. A vast majority of packages were delivered by 10:30 a.m., and a vast majority of package pickups were called in after 3 p.m. So between 10:30 a.m. and 3 p.m., there was a productivity gap, which created an opportunity to better utilize the existing FedEx personnel.

Gemini

The top-secret project was known internally as Gemini. Gemini would combine the advanced technology FedEx was already using to track packages with new technology that could deliver high-quality documents almost immediately.

The concept was threefold:

Gemini 1 – A customer would call FedEx, and our courier would pick up their document and transmit it to the Gemini machine nearest to their recipient. Then a FedEx courier would pick up and deliver it to the recipient. All within two hours.

Gemini 2 – Either the sender or recipient would have a Gemini machine in their office. FedEx software would automatically send the document to the nearest FedEx Gemini machine where a FedEx courier would deliver it to the recipient. That service was guaranteed to happen within an hour.

Gemini 3 – Both the sender and receiver would have a Gemini machine and send documents directly to each other instantaneously.

Gemini made good sense but was complicated. The opportunity was considered urgent and needed to be kept secret from our competition. Unfortunately, the current employees were left in the dark as well, which created a lot of uninformed speculation inside FedEx. Trying to merge a state-of-the-art, never-seen-before communication system into an established ground operation team represented a huge challenge. This also required new technicians, sales representatives, and other personnel. It was like trying to blend two very large families in a very short period of time. And, on top of that, we were in uncharted territory and the stakes were high.

As I said, it was complicated.

Gemini to ZapMail

It was exciting to be a part of something that was potentially really, really big. My job as district sales manager was to source, interview, and hire the electronic product-dedicated sales force to service Tennessee, Mississippi, Louisiana, Oklahoma, and Arkansas. At least as important as hiring the right people who had been successful in the electronic communication field was establishing a positive relationship with the existing FedEx sales force.

At an all-employee live and satellite meeting in July 1984, FedEx formally unveiled the secret Gemini project. The new product was named ZapMail.

ZapMail was going to change the way people did business, again.

I assumed that all FedEx employees would be supportive and thrilled about the newest product and would embrace the new ZapMail people. However, that is not exactly the way we were accepted by the FedEx employees in the field.

Many employees did not understand why FedEx was expanding and spending money at the rate that ZapMail required. After all, the overnight letter was still the most profitable product and continued to grow at a nice rate. However, the rate of growth of the FedEx overnight letter was camouflaging the exploding rate of the same-day transmission market.

In addition, the established FedEx sales force was fearful that ZapMail would dilute their overnight-letter customers. The ground operations couriers were not really looking for things to fill their productivity gap. Many of the local management teams were not happy about the secretive new division that was impacting their bonuses.

You could not blame any of them. Each of those groups was evaluating the start-up based on the impact that it could have on their operations; it impacted everyone.

Regardless, it was my job to communicate, develop trust, and deliver results so that the existing sales teams could understand our mission. We hoped they would choose to get onboard and help us make ZapMail successful. I flew all over the country delivering internal presentations about ZapMail. In most of the meetings, that message was not accepted with open arms and enthusiasm. We were considered a threat to the successful company that they had built.

At one meeting in Miami, the sales force from three or four districts was in attendance. The room was filled with about 60 people. When I began my presentation, the reception I received was brutal. One person would say something negative about ZapMail, another would try to one-up the previous comment, and then others would jump on the bandwagon.

After listening to the same concerns and complaints for quite a while, one district manager stood up and said, "Wait. Give him a chance to talk. He did not create ZapMail. If you have a problem with our new product, talk to Fred Smith." That helped settle the emotions bubbling in the room. The manager who stood up was Madeline LeBlanc from Memphis.

The reception at those communication meetings was startling. I assumed that everyone would be supportive of what we were trying to accomplish, but it wasn't so.

To the long-time FedEx representative's defense, our division had proven that we knew how to spend money, but there had been no evidence that we knew how to make money.

After that meeting in Miami, I flew to New Orleans to deliver the same presentation to another sales group. On that flight, I was bent over with my head between my hands and was reflecting on the situation that I had unexpectantly been thrown into. An older woman sitting next to me asked, "Son, is there anything that I can do for you?" I did not realize I looked so distraught. I gathered myself and thanked her for offering, but all was okay.

On to the next meeting.

The ZapMail experience was the second time in my career that I thought I was at my very best. I enjoyed hiring a brand-new sales team – it was similar to what I had done at Xerox. Even though the communication meetings were tough, I enjoyed the challenge. We were not shackled by unreasonable budgets – FedEx's core business was paying all of our bills. Our team was selling the most dynamic concept of its time. For two years, our district led the country in every measurement. It was a once-in-a-lifetime opportunity … if it worked.

From a product performance perspective, it wasn't going so well. The long-term success of ZapMail depended upon satellite transmission. The original ZapMail network was

The original
ZapMailer

hooked up to landlines – telephone lines. The plan was to launch the satellite and then disconnect the landlines. We were anxiously awaiting the launch of our own satellite.

NEC (Japan) was the manufacturer of the ZapMailer. The specifications that FedEx provided them was for packet-switching satellite transmission. By design, those transmissions were not able to communicate with existing facsimile machines. Our window of opportunity was closing as fax machines were becoming more affordable and common in business.

FedEx believed that we should own both ends of the communication network, just like we owned both ends of the package delivery business. Once we had our satellite, we would be able to deliver a service better than any competitor. However, using the landline transmission, we did not have a competitive edge and we experienced major quality and reliability issues.

The Space Shuttle Explosion
On January 28, 1986, everything changed.

Shortly after takeoff, the space shuttle Challenger tragically exploded in flight. This tragedy led to the grounding of the shuttle fleet for two-and-a-half years. Included in the grounded fleet was the shuttle that would have been sending the FedEx satellite into space.

For all intents and purposes, the ZapMail project ended on that day. In March 1986, FedEx ceased taking orders for ZapMailers while working on correcting the landline ZapMail issues and researching alternatives for our resources.

The Electronic Product Division employed hundreds of people in ZapCentral, the customer call center, which was receiving an earful from our customers every day. ZapMail had more than 600 sales reps. All told, the ZapMail team was about 2,000 people. Some of the alternatives that were considered would patch up the service for a while, but our window of opportunity was only open a crack by that time.

FedEx had spent more than a dozen years developing trust with their customers. ZapMail's service failures were putting at risk FedEx's reputation as the most dependable service organization in the world. Our division had already lost $200 million up to that point.

In October 1986, FedEx discontinued the ZapMail service and wrote off a loss of more than $300 million.

What If …

When FedEx began, Fred Smith had a vision that very few people could see. It almost failed, but he was able to sustain the company long enough to be one of the greatest success stories of my lifetime. His vision of ZapMail was just as clear for him to see. He knew that it had the potential to become a new FedEx inside of an already existing successful company. Most employees and investors could only see the profits hemorrhaging each quarter.

The failure to successfully launch our satellite was the fatal blow. We ran out of time.

Who knows what might have been? The most prominent electronic mail device in 1984 was Telex. If our satellite had been launched as scheduled, it could have opened the door for FedEx to become the data communication network of the 21st century. We would have certainly had that opportunity.

Everything that Fred Smith visualized happened within a few years of the ZapMail failure … but FedEx did not participate in it the way he had visualized.

FedEx emerged from the ZapMail experience even stronger than before. Ironically, a large influence on the growth of FedEx has been the emergence of electronic commerce and online shopping. The product mix has successfully shifted from moving information to moving products. FedEx will continue to do well.

In the history books and in most people's eyes, ZapMail was a colossal failure. However, I would not trade the experience for anything. It was my most exciting business experience. We were an early adapter to the cutting edge of technology. I was able to convince some talented people to join us in trying to change the way people did business. I learned the complexity of human emotions tied to a company the employees loved. I was able to experience what it meant for a company to live by its corporate values, even when things didn't work out like everyone hoped and dreamed. I experienced business failure for the first time and witnessed Fred Smith, Jim Barksdale, Tom Oliver, and the rest of the senior leaders lead FedEx through adversity with class and dignity.

Meanwhile, at Home …

I don't remember how or when I told Karen that our division was folding. I am sure I warned her along the way. She had her hands full at home with Jennifer, 7, and Kimberly, 4.

Karen was pregnant when ZapMail shut down. About six months into her pregnancy, she developed placenta previa where the baby's placenta covers the mom's cervix, resulting in severe bleeding. The doctors put her on bed rest for a couple of months. My sister Evelyn and my mom came and stayed with us to provide relief, but things were stressful. The doctors did not want Karen to do any activity.

When it was close to time for our baby to be born, she was admitted to the hospital. The doctors had her rest with her head well below her feet for a day. When the time came for our baby to be delivered, the birth was smooth and without any unexpected challenges.

Jennifer, Kim, and Michael
(1987)

Michael David was born on October 20, 1986. My girls had a baby brother. Karen and I had a little boy, and both mom and baby were healthy. We were blessed.

That period of my life was stressful for sure. When Michael arrived healthy, most of the stress evaporated. Even with the potential loss of my job, times were good.

My reflections on the ZapMail experience are all positive. I was blessed to be a part of something that could have been really big. Even though the venture failed, it was three years of learning how to deal with adversity, which I would draw upon years later in my own company.

Your Grace of Risk Applied

Whenever a company writes off $300 million, you know it must be the result of a major risk that did not work out. Most of us will never have the opportunity to make a decision to take a financial risk like that one.

However, there is another risk that you have the opportunity to take.

In this chapter, do you remember the ZapMail meeting in Miami? One person after another stood up and voiced their opinion. None of those people took a risk. They each expressed the same opinions. It was easy to be the next person to stand and say the same thing in a different way. I do not remember any of the names of those people who were piling on and beating that dead horse.

The person whom I *do* remember from that meeting was Madeline LeBlanc. There were a couple of managers in the meeting who joined in on their team's emotional outbursts. There were a couple of managers who chose to remain quiet.

Madeline was probably the youngest manager in the room. She did not jump on the bashwagon. She took a stand even though it was not popular among her constituents. Why did she do that? No one would have thought less of her if she had joined in with the popular bashing. She took a risk and stood up because it was the right thing to do.

What would you do? Would you pile on or would you be standing up alone for what you thought was right?

Taking a risk rarely involves money. More times than not, it involves standing for your beliefs. I hope you will make the decision to know your beliefs well enough that you will stand up for them, even when you are standing alone.

Those years at FedEx taught me a lot. They were not easy lessons, but I'm glad I learned from them. The content of challenges changes, but the process by which you and I deal with them remains the same.

eight

Grace of Growth

Post-ZapMail – Adversity to Opportunity

---

*Press on. Your defining moment may arrive
just when you feel surrounded by adversity.*

FedEx was a great company, but the demise of ZapMail was
a supreme test of its foundation. Fred Smith had built the
company upon a corporate philosophy of People, Service,
and Profit (P-S-P) being the three most important priorities
of the company. He frequently communicated that the
priorities came in that order – take care of our people, they
will deliver an impeccable service to our customers, who in
turn will provide us the profits necessary for our continued
growth. Taking care of our people came first. In addition,
FedEx had also established a no-layoff policy.

The P-S-P philosophy and no-layoff policy were easy to say
and do during good times. But, when ZapMail failed, there
were more than 2,000 employees whose jobs were eliminated
almost overnight. At that time, the total number of FedEx
employees was about 20,000. Over 10 percent of the company
had been displaced.

One of the attributes I admired about Fred Smith's leadership was that he steadfastly focused on the long-term objectives without submitting to the short-term fluctuations and pressures of the business. FedEx, under his direction, made the decision that the company would live up to its stated values even though it would have a huge negative impact on short-term profits. That decision took some guts. After all, who would have blamed him if he decided that keeping all those extra people, including me, would jeopardize the rest of the company? No one.

His direction was to find comparable positions for those who wanted to stay. A large percentage of the ZapMail people left FedEx at that time, but many decided to continue to stay. I am glad I did.

The mainstream FedEx sales force was well-established. With the ZapMail sales team being melded into the existing sales force, we were adding almost 600 new people – basically doubling its size. The ZapMail team, who came to FedEx to be part of the Electronic Products Division that no longer existed, were not happy campers, although most were grateful to have a job. The existing FedEx sales team were not happy campers, either. In fact, there were not many happy campers among the sales force at that time. The merging of the sales forces was an emotional, logistical, and physical challenge.

My situation was similar to what was happening all over the country. I lived in Memphis. FedEx already had a district in Memphis. FedEx already had sales representatives in every city where my team was located. The ZapMail people were the ones invading into established territories and relationships. Obviously, it was not an ideal situation.

Madeline LeBlanc, the same person who stood up for me in the Miami meeting a couple of years earlier, was the existing district manager in Memphis. Our task was clear – take the combined personnel and resources of our two divisions and divide them into two new districts. That sounds easy, but we were both protective of our people. There were some of her representatives that I did not care to have on my team, and there were some of mine that she would not be thrilled managing.

We agreed to meet at my office and begin the merging process. We discussed the situation and began exploring the options available. Some of the decisions were easy because of logistics. The representatives who lived in the same city would be on one team. Our major challenge was making sure that one district was not stacked with all the best people and one district had all the people whose performances were not so great. After coming up with the parameters we were going to use for the merger, we outlined the teams on flip charts and began adjusting where needed.

We arrived at a mutually agreed-upon result. We had agreed up front that the objective was to have the districts equal so that either of us would take either team. We would then flip a coin to determine which team we would have. When the process was completed, I believed that Madeline, the current district manager, should have her pick. After we agreed that we each would take either team, I asked her to take her pick. She did. That is how we merged the ZapMail and FedEx districts into one semi-happy family.

Dallas

When I left Xerox to work at FedEx, I believed that I would finish my career in Memphis. The FedEx corporate office was there and I believed there would be plenty of opportunities in the aggressive company. I had been offered a promotion to Chicago within the company, but I was not interested in making that move. The only place outside of Memphis that appealed to me was Dallas, which was closer to both Karen and my families.

The Dallas district was of significant importance to FedEx. We had a good presence there, and several of FedEx's largest customers were in the Dallas-Fort Worth area. In early December 1986, the district manager in Dallas was fired. I immediately made it known that I was interested in the lateral transfer if FedEx would pick up my relocation expenses. They said okay.

Family photo (1989)

Karen and I went to Dallas to find a place to live. We decided to build a house in the suburb of DeSoto. When we bought the house at 1435 Mosslake, it was in the framing stage of construction. We took the girls and baby Michael to see the house. Nine-year-old Jennifer ran all through the house and began crying … she could not find any place to hide. We assured her that there would be plenty of places to hide when we moved into our new home. Kimberly would not say anything and wouldn't let go of her mom. Michael accepted the move the best. He was only three months old.

We moved to the Dallas area in February 1987.

The Dallas district had some good, solid representatives. The relationships with the ground operations personnel were positive, and the Dallas ZapMail personnel merged smoothly with the traditional FedEx sales group. It was a great place for me to absorb the impact of the ZapMail failure and begin my new career inside the mainstream of FedEx. Things were stable for a change.

In 1988, my career took a quantum leap forward. FedEx decided to pursue the Malcolm Baldrige Award that was presented by the Department of Commerce to the best quality companies in the U.S. At that time, no service company had ever won the award. The criteria to apply for the award was incredibly tough and was written primarily for manufacturing companies because the award weighted statistical process control as the main criteria. When FedEx decided to pursue the award, it was given a major priority within the company.

One of the first actions was to train our sales force on quality, which consisted primarily of problem-solving techniques. The techniques were similar to some of the courses that I taught while at Xerox. I volunteered to take a lead in training our sales force. That was a major step for me. It imbedded the FedEx culture into my philosophy while allowing me to pursue my passion of training and personal development. The training job was in addition to my normal district manager activities, but that was okay. Our district was running smoothly at that time.

Another Reorganization

Another major break for me happened in May 1990 when FedEx announced a major sales force reorganization. In this reorganization, I was given the opportunity to become a region manager responsible for 12 districts. I could also remain in Dallas. There was a significant amount of travel involved, but for the third time in my career, I felt like I was the right person in the right place at the right time. With the new organization, I had the opportunity to impact more people and expand my philosophy of personal development into a broader group.

One of the programs that my manager, Wallace Moorehand, and I instituted was a dedicated personal development week for each district manager. It was affectionately known as Hell Week. I would take two managers at a time for a week. They would be given 10 books to read during that week. Every day they were given two books and we would meet at lunch and the end of the day to discuss their thoughts about the book they had read that morning or afternoon. The books were on time management, presentations, leadership, management, personal development, recognition, coaching, and problem solving. After reading all of the books, the district manager would create an action plan to present to his team on what they could expect from him.

It was a strenuous but valuable exercise for both the district manager and me. I would learn more about their leadership philosophy during that dedicated week than I could in five years of observation. It also reinforced my leadership philosophies that would eventually become the cornerstone of my own business.

Malcolm Baldrige Award

In 1990, FedEx won the Malcolm Baldrige National Quality Award, becoming the first service organization to win the award. Winning was a big deal. Fred Smith, Jim Barksdale, and Tom Oliver were obsessed with customer satisfaction. The major breakthrough for winning the Malcolm Baldrige Award was when our executive leadership created a systematic way to measure our performance, called SQI – Service Quality

Indicators. We used advanced technology to measure our performance daily against the most important expectations of our customers. The SQI process and the tracking of it were brilliant. We could monitor in real-time where we had issues so that we could address them before they became bigger. It was a game changer for measuring quality in the service arena.

When an organization applies for the Malcolm Baldrige Award, they must agree up front that if they win, they will share their story with other U.S. organizations. I was involved in the application for the award and I had a good base of information about our system. I volunteered to become a Malcolm Baldrige spokesman for FedEx.

I had to learn how to become a professional public speaker quickly. I enrolled in an intense two-week speaker's workshop in Atlanta conducted by a company named SpeakEasy. The crash course taught me the fundamentals of how to present a professional speech. It was a great investment of my time and FedEx's money. Every talk was videotaped and critiqued. The feedback was excruciating. I loved it.

Shortly after my training, I began presenting the FedEx story all over the country. It was fun and fulfilling, just like my professional speaking career would be a few years later.

My first big speech was at an Exxon managers' meeting in Houston. I thought the 500-person audience was a huge crowd. Sitting behind me on the stage where I was speaking was one of the fathers of the quality movement. It was pretty intimidating.

A couple of weeks later, my definition of huge crowd was elevated to a new level. One of my district managers asked me to speak at a City of Austin employee conference. When I arrived in Austin the night before the speech, he and I went to check out the facility. I was expecting a few hundred people, but the meeting was in the municipal auditorium and the audience would be 7,000 people. Aside from the gigantic audience, it was to be broadcast live on public television.

Yikes.

In preparation for that speech, I had decided to try something that I had seen Jim Barksdale do once to connect with his audience. I was dressed in a suit with a tie. About five minutes into the talk, I took off my tie, then my jacket, and the audience could then see that I was wearing a FedEx courier uniform – epaulets and all. The surprise twist was rewarded by an immediate ovation, which inspired me and probably helped keep my audience awake for the remainder of the one-hour presentation. Looking back at that video, the presentation was pretty darn good. I don't believe that anyone could tell how terrified I was.

My days at FedEx were awesome. I learned a lot. I could stretch myself into many areas that were not comfortable for me. I had fun.

I had the privilege of being one of the few people on the planet to work for two Malcolm Baldrige Award-winning companies while at Xerox and FedEx. I believed that my next career move needed to be to a smaller company where I could use what I had learned from those two great organizations.

I began to get an itch to move on even though I still loved FedEx. I guess I had a 10-year itch since that is approximately the amount of time I spent in each of my other two organizations. It would have been a lot easier to not scratch the itch rather than make my next move. But, at age 39, I made the decision to move on and begin writing my next career chapter.

***

Your Grace of Growth Applied

The way that FedEx responded to adversity was incredibly admirable. I will be forever grateful. FedEx made the decision to take care of its people long before the ZapMail crisis. Their priorities were clearly established. There was no suddenness of choice. Their choice to maintain their values trumped all their other options. They had no idea about the commitment or resources that would be required to implement their values.

What would you do? Do you have your personal and professional values clearly stated so that you can be free to implement the decision that you have already made? Maybe it is time for you to eliminate any suddenness of choice and to put some thought into the values that you will live by, regardless of the challenges that are thrown your way.

Maybe it's as simple as choosing time with family over other options. Maybe it's making a commitment to friends or family that might require time, resources, and finances. Maybe it's being a person of integrity, come what may.

Somewhere along the way you will be faced with adversity. No one is immune. Your gut check comes when things go wrong – an unexpected event that hits you squarely between the eyes. After the shock of an unexpected event, you have to make a choice. You can choose to become mired in the quicksand of self-pity – immobilized, stuck, and unable to move ahead. Or you can make the choice to live your values and attack the adversity that you are facing.

Adversity will grind you down or polish you up. Which will you choose?

nine

Grace of Tough Learning

Cheerleading – No Rah-Rah

Things are not always the way they appear.
Grace upon grace was disguised for a while.

It was in the spring of 1993 when I received a call from a headhunter. It was not unusual to receive a call of this nature, but this one was intriguing because it was an executive vice president for a medium-size organization … and it was in Dallas. Bingo. It sounded like a great next career move for me.

Not so fast, my friend.

The organization was the National Spirit Group (NSG), the holding company for Cheerleader & Danzteam and National Cheerleaders Association (NCA). I did not know anything about cheerleading. Even though my high school girlfriend was a cheerleader, it did not exactly provide me a lot of applicable experience in that arena.

1995 NSG catalog

The recruiter believed that I was the perfect candidate to run the apparel division. NSG had recently recovered from Chapter 11 re-organization and he described the company as "stable and ready for growth." The owner of the company was convinced that things had turned around and that "we just need a steady hand in leadership." I became excited about the opportunity to provide that steady hand while leading sales and marketing.

Karen was on board with the job change. Like me, she had been "wowed" by the owner, who may have been the smoothest salesperson that I had ever seen. He was charismatic and exhibited a kind and optimistic demeanor during every interview. He was selling and I was buying.

The only red flag that was waving was from my best friend, Louis Krueger. Louis had inside information from someone who previously worked for the owner. Louis sternly warned me to stay away and told me not to touch it with a 10-foot pole. That was not what I wanted to hear, so I didn't listen. I rationalized that the information Louis had was from a disgruntled former employee. In my mind, there was no way that the owner could possibly be in the picture that Louis was painting. No way.

My first day at NSG was eye-opening. Shocking. Alarming. Disturbing.

NSG needed much more than a steady hand. When I arrived home after my first day there, I walked in and asked Karen to come to our bedroom, away from the children for a minute. When she entered the bedroom, I was visibly upset. I shut the door and told her that I had made the biggest mistake of our lives. She was shocked. How could it be so different than we thought? She listened to me and assured me that everything would be okay. She encouraged me that maybe the reason I took that job was to use my skills to make it better. Yeah, right. I was scared and embarrassed. I called Louis that evening and told him that he and his friend were right.

I left a wonderful, secure position and walked into a hornet's nest full of problems. Our on-time delivery of cheerleader uniforms was less than 30 percent. Our receivables were largely uncollectable because of our performance. The sales team was not communicating with the manufacturing plant. Customer service was fighting the same types of fires that ZapCentral fought … on the other end of every call was an irate customer.

The atmosphere at the company was toxic. Customers were upset, employees were upset, investors were upset. No one was happy. I had no choice other than to get to work on the problems.

I immediately learned that the cheerleading apparel business is tough.

First, all over the country, tryouts for cheerleaders happen within a two-month period in the spring. Ninety percent of the orders for their uniforms are placed during that time. When production issues surfaced, we would not realize it until it had already impacted almost every order.

Second, every school needs their cheerleading uniforms at the same time in late summer before the first football game. All the orders had to be produced and shipped at about the same time. In addition, the accounts receivable came in at one time, long after the expenses of making the uniforms.

Third, cheerleader uniforms are the true definition of mass customization. Every girl has a unique body size. Every school has a unique mascot. Every school's color palettes are uniquely different. The average order size was less than 20. All of those factors added to the challenge of producing the correct uniform and creating satisfied customers.

Fourth, most cheerleaders are in seventh through twelfth grades. From the time that the orders are submitted in the spring, their body sizes have changed before the orders are delivered in the fall.

Fifth, many of the sales representatives were seasonal employees.

Each of those problems had the potential to be deadly. Strangely, my experience was a good fit to help identify and solve some of those problems.

The owner was a marketing genius. He had made a ton of money in the school ring business. He knew the ins and outs of selling to schools. He was the inventor of the "fly away" cheerleading skirt that would become a best-selling design. He thought of it while he was sitting in his car while going through a car wash. He noticed the large strips of rubber that would go back and forth to scrub his car. He thought, "Why not manufacture a cheerleading skirt that flies away like that?" That is how the most popular skirt in cheerleading began.

He also invented an elastic area on the cheerleader top that would stretch to fit if the girl's size had changed after being measured. That is how his mind worked, always searching for a new and better idea.

However, managing and leading were not his expertise. He told me that before I came on board, but he didn't tell me that he would still try to get into everything. The owner was acutely dyslexic. That made it difficult for him to keep things in sequence. He could remember everything he experienced, but he could not read a report or remember facts that he did not personally experience.

Even with the difficulties he experienced, he was brilliant. However, two hours of the owner visiting the company would require at least two days for things to settle down and recover. He told everyone what they wanted to hear even if it contradicted what he had just told someone else. If we could have caged the owner into the marketing, cataloging, and creative areas, it would have been a win for everyone.

One Sunday afternoon, less than two months after I began at NSG, the owner called a meeting with me and our CFO, Mark Shakleford. Mark was a good, loyal, and smart soldier, but the owner would beat on him like a dusty rug. The news that day was bad. We were in a crisis. Our cash flow had dried up. It was so bad that the owner asked if I had cashed my payroll check. I had.

Filing Chapter 11 for the second time would have been disastrous. We had several hundred employees' careers at risk. Mark suggested that he could sell our receivables for a percentage of its worth. The owner would have to go back to the investors for more money. If I was not able to fix our production and sales problems, it would all be short term anyway.

Time to Go to Work

The first issue I attacked was the timing of the orders. I called the sudden influx of orders a mountain. We needed to build a ramp up that mountain.

Most schools have new cheerleader tryout dates in the early spring. Their uniform orders are placed only after the tryouts. However, if we could get 5 percent of our orders to come in January and February, we could begin manufacturing and determine where our issues might be before we hit the mountain. Believing what gets rewarded gets done, I incented our representatives and our customers to buy early. For orders in January and February, we paid the reps a significant bonus and provided discounts to the schools. We didn't need a huge amount of orders to accomplish our objectives. The strategy worked to the level we needed.

The second issue I had to attack was streamlining our sales and manufacturing process. The owner had already provided our representatives with laptops for order taking. That was a forward-thinking, good move at the time. The laptops were being utilized for documenting the order instead of transmitting the order. The representatives would print the orders and fax them to customer service, which would input the orders to the factory. That system was inefficient and unreliable. The customer service agents could misread or miss-stroke the information as easy as they could get it right. Manufacturing had been blamed for most of the issues, but the real issue was order-input integrity. We equipped the laptops with modems to connect directly with the factory, which eliminated the middle step. It sounds so obvious now, but it was a major change in the way our representatives did business.

The third issue was the productivity of customer service. A large percentage of the calls they were taking, and an even larger percentage of their time on the phone, was consumed by our own sales representatives. We asked our IT people to connect our sales representatives to real-time order information so that they could track and see their order progress through the manufacturing process. That solved the need for our reps to be on the phone with customer service to find out the information that was now available directly to them.

The same program that was created by IT allowed the representative and their manager to track sales performance in real time. We even used the same term we had at Xerox – the SAX report.

We made significant progress that year. Our on-time delivery rates escalated to over 70 percent; not great but a vast improvement.

The next year, we improved even more. By that time, the owner was desperately trying to sell the company. I never knew all the things that were going on behind the scenes, but the information that I was receiving was, in my opinion, deceitful to the potential buyers and not favorable toward me.

By that time, I was worn out with the owner. We had a tough row to hoe together and we did reasonably well. I had signed a three-year agreement. On the first day of the fourth year, I resigned.

Looking back, Karen was right. The experience that I brought to NSG did make it better. NSG made me better, too. I learned how to keep my cool through a crisis, utilize direct marketing, develop catalogs, write copy, and many other things that would benefit me later in my career.

I learned a lot of tough lessons from the owner.

When I left NSG, I joined Optel, a Canadian cable and phone company. They had offered me a $150,000 salary plus a large bonus to work for them. That was a lot of money in 1995. I was never overly enthused about the limited market they served, which was large apartment complexes. I was not a good fit in their Canadian culture where I spent a vast majority of my time in unproductive meetings. I worked at Optel for only six months.

I then took the big plunge to begin my own company.

Your Grace of Tough Learning Applied

Tough learning was not fun for me. It probably would not be fun for you, either. My friend had information that I chose to ignore. My ego convinced me that I knew more than my best friend. I only saw what I wanted to see and heard what I wanted to hear. I hope that you never make that mistake.

I learned a lot at NSG. My experience there made me a better person. The most important lesson I learned was to protect my integrity. I really wanted to resign soon after discovering the harsh reality of the situation I inherited. That would have been my easiest route, but I would be bailing on much more than just my word. People were dependent on me to make things better.

I reluctantly fulfilled my three-year commitment and was able to use my grace of tough learning throughout the rest of my career.

I also discovered that regardless of the situation I was in, I still needed people to trust me.

There are very few people in your life whom you can totally trust. Think about it. Stop right now and make a list of the people whom you can trust with everything. They may be family members, friends, business associates, teachers, clergy, or community leaders – they can be anyone, as long as you trust them. Write their names:

____

____

____

If you are like most, even with 7.6 billion people to choose from, your list is pretty short.

Now ask yourself how many people would write your name on their list?

If you lose trust, nothing else really matters. You see examples on the news every day of people who lost everything they worked for because of an integrity breach. That is an expensive price to pay.

It simply makes no difference how great your intentions are. Without trust, there is no foundation for a successful long-term relationship. Protect your integrity like it is one of your most prized possessions, because that is exactly what it is.

I believe that everyone will face tough learning somewhere along the way. When you find yourself in an uncomfortable, difficult situation, remember the advice of Mother Teresa of

Calcutta, who said, "When it is hard, remember we are not called to be successful but to be faithful. Let no one ever come to you without leaving better and happier."

While I was experiencing tough learning, it was not the time for me to surrender, although it was tempting. I found that it was the time for me to press on and help others who were going through their tough learning with me. Being my best in the future depended on me making the best of my tough learning from my past.

You may discover, as I did, that being faithful to keep moving toward becoming the person you want to be and bringing others with you will be your ultimate measure of success.

ten

Grace of Perseverance

CornerStone and Divine Intervention

The business plan seemed so logical.
I could not understand why the business struggled
and was on the verge of shutting down.
God's plan was a lot better.

Throughout my career, I was passionate about professional development. I observed for many years that most organizations did not have the time or resources to provide great management or leadership training. My experience while at NSG and Optel reflected the same observation – there was no pre-management training at any level. What typically happened was that the best salesperson was promoted to sales management. The best accountant was promoted to head the accounting department. The best follower was promoted to lead. In some cases, it worked out, but in many cases the skill sets of individual performance did not transfer to leadership.

I didn't consider creating a training organization until two friends from my FedEx days approached me with the idea of starting a training and development company together. The timing was good for me. I was not thrilled with Optel and I had stashed some money away to begin something on my own if the right opportunity ever came along.

Jim Wallace lived in Memphis and was a seasoned human resource professional. Ken Carnes lived in Houston. I had worked with Ken at FedEx and NSG before he became an executive in the personnel placement business. We knew each other well and each of us had a deep, personal passion about professional development.

Jim, Ken, and I met on nights and weekends for a couple of months and created a business plan that would become CornerStone Leadership Institute. The three of us brought different skills into the business. We were a good fit, both personally and professionally. Our business model was going to be similar to Brian Tracy's model. Brian was an acquaintance of mine and he provided some good advice and direction. One thing he neglected to tell me was that it took him five years to get his business off the ground. Maybe he did tell me and I did not want to hear it, or perhaps it slipped my memory. Regardless, Jim, Ken, and I worked together and created a comprehensive business plan.

Our plan was to provide leadership training … focusing on small- and medium-size organizations. The vehicle we would use would be one-, two-, or three-day workshops in different cities. We would start off in Dallas, Houston, San Antonio, and Austin – following the Southwest Airlines' model – and then expand as we grew.

Creating content was the easiest part of the plan. Each of us had delivered leadership content for years and we were all dedicated students of leadership. Our marketing strategy would utilize direct mail. Our administrator would be Sherri Durham, who had worked with me for several years in three different companies. Jim had a graphic designer friend who created our logo and branding. Ken had an attorney friend to draw up our bylaws and articles of incorporation. A friend of mine became our accountant.

We created a best, most likely, and worst-case scenario. We presented our plan to another friend, a senior executive at BankUnited. He was impressed with our well-thought-out business plan.

I invested $40,000 and was the CEO and largest stakeholder. Ken and Jim invested smaller amounts and were minority stakeholders. We provided Sherri several hundred CornerStone shares with no monetary investment from her. BankUnited loaned us $75,000. Ken, Jim, and I were each liable for the full amount.

On December 4, 1996, our articles of incorporation were filed in the state of Texas.

We were in business. In January, our direct-mail campaign would begin. Our seminars would launch in February. The brochures our designer created were spectacular – the highest quality. The image we portrayed was that of a large, well-established organization.

Our content was good. Ken and I would be the facilitators, and we both had a wealth of experience presenting. We were ready. Everything was in place. This rocket was about to be launched.

We dropped our brochures in the mail and waited for the calls and faxes to start coming in to register for one of the upcoming seminars. It was disappointing when only a few people registered for our first public seminar. We filled the hotel room primarily with friends and family, but there was not a lot of revenue generated. The feedback was good. In our first seminar, over 90 percent of the participants said they would recommend it to others – thank you, friends and family.

We experienced similar results in Houston and Austin. We canceled San Antonio. The business plan that looked so good on paper was not producing. One of my advisers in the planning stage advised that we needed to double our expenses and split our profits in half … that is what happens to most start-ups. He was right.

We did not have enough capital to continue very long. Ken and I both invested more money into CornerStone. Jim was not delivering content or actively involved in the business. He wanted to cut his losses and get out. That is what he did.

Ken continued working with CornerStone for a few more months, but then he had to leave for a more stable income.

I was not aware that Sherri was having some personal problems. She left to go to the dentist one Friday and never returned.

It was lonely at CornerStone Leadership Institute, but I was not ready to throw in the towel. I was able to land some small consulting gigs that barely kept me in the game. Every month I paid the CornerStone note. Financially and emotionally, things were real fragile.

Write a Book

Joe Miles was one of my best friends. We were golf buddies and our girls played on the same soccer teams for several years. Joe suggested that I call Rick Butts, a consultant for the company where Joe worked. Joe thought that Rick had been where I was and he might be able to provide me some advice.

Why not? I had nothing to lose.

I called Rick Butts. After explaining my situation to him, he understood what I was going through. He had also been there. He asked some questions and then said, "You have to write a book. You have had a great career, but nobody knows anything about you. Write a book. It will be better than any sales brochure you could create." Well, that sounded good, but I had never considered writing a book. I asked Rick to explain the book he wrote. His book, *The Safari Adventure,* was a story about things that went wrong on a safari. The people had to work together to survive. The book demonstrated the problem-solving techniques that he taught. That made sense to me.

After my call to Rick, I was mowing my yard and feeling sorry for myself. I didn't have a safari adventure experience to write about. After a few minutes of self-pity, I began thinking about experiences that I did have that could translate into a book. It then came to me that I knew more than most about golf and I had studied leadership my entire professional career. Why not put those two things together? I began writing a story about a golf match and how the lessons learned during that match could apply to business.

When the first draft was ready, I asked Karen, Kim, and Michael to come to the table to hear my story. I read it out loud to them. They tried to be nice and supportive, but I could tell that they were in shock. It was written on a yellow legal pad and the story was weak, to say the least. I remember one of them saying, "I am not sure. I think it needs some work." Reflecting on the original draft, that may be the kindest comment in history.

I continued to work on the book, which would ultimately become *Birdies, Pars, and Bogeys … Leadership Lessons From the Links.* After several weeks, I had a draft that was decent. I did not know what to do with the book and went to a book printer to ask questions. There I met Gil Pitts, who put me in touch with a book designer, DeFae Weaver, and a cover designer, Keith Crabtree. After working with them, Gil printed the book. The first print run was 2,000 copies.

In the meantime, Michael was playing on a Little League baseball team. I was talking to one of his coaches and told him that I was writing a book. He said that he worked for the largest distributor of books for airport gift shops. I had no idea. He said to let him know when I had the book printed and he would pass it up the chain in his company. I did and he did. They gave me a purchase order for almost every book I had printed. The book sold well. Then, the Tournament Players Club (TPC) golf stores picked the book up for their airport shops.

Rick Butts was right. I was being interviewed on television and receiving some nice publicity. I was a published author who had much more credibility all of a sudden.

Tough Decisions

I was still struggling financially. Before I began CornerStone, I had three buckets of money. The first bucket had been set aside for investing in my own business if the opportunity ever came my way. The money was largely from my stock in NSG.

That bucket was bone dry. The second bucket was emergency funds that I had put away for our family. That bucket was almost empty. The third bucket contained my retirement funds. I was looking into that bucket and had almost rationalized that it would be okay to dip into that bucket as well.

I landed a few small consulting contracts, which helped a little. The book income helped as well, but I was not making as much money as our family needed. I had to make some humbling and difficult decisions.

First, the monthly CornerStone note was a burden. I was paying the note each month even though my original CornerStone partners and I were equally liable. I called Jim and Ken and explained my financial situation. I proposed that I would continue paying the note, pardon them of their obligation, and in return they would release their shares of stock back to me. They agreed. I then owned 100 percent of the CornerStone stock. At that time, the stock was worth less than the stamp they had to lick to put on the envelope to send the papers to me.

That did not solve my immediate financial problem, but it did provide me full equity if CornerStone were to ever succeed.

The second decision I had to make meant having one of the toughest conversations of my life. Karen knew that we were struggling, but I had protected her from the details of our financial situation. I could not hide those specifics any longer.

One night when she came to bed, I told her that we needed to talk. I explained in detail where we were financially. I asked her if she would go back to work for a while so we could have some steady income and health benefits.

Karen had been a stay-at-home mom for 16 years. She had been involved in every one of our kid's activities. I always said that she had a "V" printed on her forehead for all to see that she would volunteer for anything. She had been in her element and was the best. I was asking her to give that up. It was the most humiliating conversation that I have ever had. I was embarrassed and ashamed.

After a few seconds of silence, she said that she would start substituting and that she might be able to get a full-time teaching position the next school year. It was like she knew it was coming, but she never told me that she expected that to happen.

She was right – she substituted and then was hired full time in the fall. That relieved some of the financial pressure.

Write Another Book

While at FedEx, I had purchased several booklets written by Price Pritchett. Each of his booklets was brief, only 56 pages. They had some great organizational development material and catchy titles like *Business as Unusual*. His marketing method was direct mail. He would send free copies of his booklet to organizations and they would order directly from his company. That model made sense to me. He sold the booklets for $9.95, and I estimated that they cost him less than a dollar each to print and mail.

I had learned a lot about direct mail and graphic design while at NSG. I thought I would try the Pritchett model. My due diligence on Pritchett's business model consisted of me reading in the back of one of his books how many books he had sold and how many clients he served. That information was impressive and I thought it would be worth a shot.

I needed to develop new content that would be applicable to businesses of all sizes. When I made the speech in the courier uniform in Austin, it was interesting how people seemed to have paid more attention while I was speaking to them from the eyes of a courier instead of an executive. That moment stuck with me. So, I began to develop a book from the perspective of employees. I hit on a good title: *Listen Up, Leader! Pay attention, improve, and guide.* The 56-page booklet addressed several suggestions that employees would like to tell their employer.

I had 7,000 books printed. Five thousand of the books were printed with a false cover that would serve as a marketing piece on one side and the address label for the U.S. mail on the other side. I contacted a couple of friends in the human resources field and asked them which magazine was the most respected and informative for human resource professionals. Both agreed that *Human Resource Executive* magazine was the gold standard. I made the decision to send 5,000 books to subscribers of *Human Resource Executive* magazine. My target audience was vice president or above of companies with 500 or more employees.

I invested about $10,000 in the experiment. My decision was based on sales numbers found in the back of a Pritchett book and the advice of a couple of human resources professionals. It was a risky experiment.

My mail house dropped the booklets into the mail. Several days passed. As I was sitting in my office alone with my fax machine, the fax machine began making a very distinctive squealing sound, alerting me that it was about to receive a transmission. A few minutes later, it spit out a completed order form from Lowe's Home Improvement. They ordered

1,600 of the books for a managers' meeting that they were having the next week. That order generated enough money to pay for the entire project. I even had money left over. I thought, "What have I got here?"

I received several more decent-size orders for *Listen Up, Leader!* I was not exactly sure where to go from there. It would be difficult for me to duplicate the content and frequency of new products like Price Pritchett was doing. I was a one-man office without the resources or structure to make that happen.

There was another company in Dallas that was duplicating the Pritchett model. The Walk The Talk Company was smaller in size than Pritchett but produced excellent content. The company was named after their best-selling book, *Walk The Talk … And Get The Results You Want.*

Eric Harvey was the owner of Walk The Talk. I called and asked if I could meet with him. He graciously agreed and we met in his office. I showed him the results I had with *Listen Up, Leader!* He immediately offered to re-publish *Listen Up, Leader!* through Walk The Talk.

Walk The Talk had an impressive, loyal customer base. Eric proposed a royalty structure that was fair and equitable. I told him that we had a deal if he shared with me his "system." Neither he nor I thought that I would have the resources to do much with that information, but I thought it would be interesting to understand how Walk The Talk worked.

We agreed that he would own the rights to *Listen Up, Leader!*, I would be paid a royalty, and more importantly, I would be involved in the Walk The Talk marketing decisions of the book.

Now What?

Listen Up, Leader! became a best-selling booklet. It sold over 250,000 copies and provided me with several speaking and consulting gigs. However, the royalties and consulting income were being consumed by my office overhead and the BankUnited note. I needed a more reliable, steady income stream.

A business associate suggested that I meet with Ed Foreman. I did not know anything about Ed, but I was told that he could be a potential mentor and maybe an investor. I researched Ed and discovered that he was the only person in history who had been a U.S. Representative in two different states – New Mexico and Texas.

I called him and we met at his Dallas office. He was gracious with his time and advice. I filled him in on my CornerStone journey. He asked, "What would you like for me to do?" I told him that I needed an infusion of cash to keep going and I would like for him to invest in CornerStone.

Ed stared at me. For what appeared to be several minutes, he did not say a word. Then, he said, "I am going to help you." I sat still. In my mind, I was anticipating how much money he wanted to invest. I was about to get a break.

Then, he went on to say, "I am not going to invest any money. You have done all of the hard work. You are on the edge of making it. You may not see it, but I can. If I invested with you, each month that you wrote me a check for the return of my investment, you would be irritated. You need to stay the course and wait for your breakthrough. It won't be long."

Well, that conversation was interesting. He was encouraging, but I walked away from his office that day with the same problem that I had when I walked in. I definitely could not see that I was on the "edge of making it." All I could see was that I was on the edge of being broke.

Rock Bottom

Moving back into corporate America was looking better each month. I was growing weary of the month-to-month expense crunch. My situation elevated in December 1998. It was around Christmastime and the BankUnited note was due to be drafted from the CornerStone account in two days. I did not have enough money in the CornerStone account to cover the draft. I took my personal credit card and swiped it into the credit card machine, which would deposit it in the CornerStone account. I inputted the amount that would cover the draft.

I broke out in a cold sweat. I had hit rock bottom and it was a sick feeling. I realized that things could not continue without some divine intervention or major changes. I could not continue to swipe my personal card to pay CornerStone bills – that was not an option.

If you have ever hit rock bottom, you know that there are no springs on the rock. It is the lowest point you can reach. That is where I was.

Divine Intervention Happened

As I was pondering my next move, I received a call from a former business acquaintance, Mark Layton. I had known Mark during my time at FedEx, where he was a client. Karen and I hosted Mark and his wife, Cherie, at the FedEx Orange Bowl and St. Jude Classic Golf Tournament. I knew him reasonably well, but we were not particularly close – in fact, I had not seen him in a few years. When I began CornerStone,

I sent a letter to several executives in Dallas whom I had done business with in the past at FedEx and NSG. Mark was on that list.

I was sitting alone in my office when Mark Layton called. Mark was the CEO of Daisytek International, a midsize company headquartered in Dallas. Daisytek began as a manufacturer of products for daisy wheel printers and had evolved into a major distributor of computer and office supplies.

After a few minutes of catching up, Mark asked me if I was available and interested in speaking at a conference his company was sponsoring in Washington, D.C., at the end of January. Of course I was. I certainly didn't have to clear my calendar – there wasn't anything on it.

The audience would be his largest customers, including HP, Xerox, 3M, and Sony. After listening to what he was wanting in a workshop, I told him that I would be honored to work with his team. In my mind I was thinking that this may be my last meeting representing CornerStone.

Little did I know what God had in store.

The workshop went well. I met with several of his customers and I enjoyed the time I spent with the Daisytek team. Shortly after my workshop at the conference, Mark said that he had received a lot of good comments and he was very pleased. He suggested that we play golf soon after we returned to Dallas from Washington, D.C.

Mark was very successful, around 40 years old, and a smart guy. I admired his accomplishments at Daisytek. He and I were both avid golfers, and we agreed on a date to get together and play.

A couple of weeks later, we met at Stonebridge Ranch Country Club, which is just north of Dallas. After warming up, we began our round. We were the only two playing and had four hours of competition and conversation ahead of us.

While playing the third hole, I asked Mark what he thought his next career move may be. He said that he had been thinking about that question for a while. He asked me if I had read the book *Halftime* by Bob Buford. I said I had and that book had a positive impact on me when I began CornerStone. The theme of the book is *how to move from success to significance.* Mark said that reading that book had encouraged him to think about how he could make his move from success to significance.

After talking several minutes about Buford's book, I told Mark that I was working on a book that would probably never be published, but I would like for him to review the manuscript. He said that he would be glad to. He asked me to send the manuscript to his office. He would get back to me with his thoughts within a couple of weeks.

The manuscript pinpointed 12 leadership principles that I thought were necessary for sustained success. You may wonder how a guy who was struggling in his business could write a book about sustained success. I wondered that as well. The reason I wrote the book was to clarify my own beliefs. I had discovered many years before that when I wrote things down, it helped me see more clearly, so that was the purpose of writing the book. I didn't have any intention of publishing the manuscript, nor did I have the resources to make it happen. It was written by me and for me. After identifying the 12 principles, I validated each principle with Scriptural references.

I sent the manuscript to Mark the following day. In about
a week, he called and said that he was prepared to provide
some feedback. We set up a meeting for the next day. I didn't
have any great expectations for the meeting other than
listening to what a smart, successful friend thought of the
concepts I was presenting.

The next day we met in his office. I immediately asked him
what he thought. Many of my thoughts expressed in the
manuscript were somewhat similar to Bob Buford's thoughts
expressed in *Halftime,* so I thought I was on safe ground with
Mark. He said that he liked the book, but he had an issue
with something that I wrote regarding money. The story that
he was referring to was in the very last chapter, so I knew that
he made it all the way through the manuscript.

I had written a story about the richest people in Chicago in
1923 and what eventually happened to each of them. By 1948,
almost every one of them died a tragic death. My inference
was that the love of money probably led to their tragedy. Mark
pushed back on that story. He said that I did not know what
caused those tragedies and that it was not necessarily money
that led to their demise. To me, what I had written was a
logical conclusion, but I told him that he was right. I did not
know if my assumption was a fact. I told him that I would take
that story out; no one else would ever see that in my writing.

I asked him if there was anything else. He said that he liked
and believed what I had written. He then said, "Would you
be willing to teach those principles to all of the managers
at Daisytek? You would need to take out the Scriptural
references but teach the principles so that our company has
a common base. We have managers in the U.S., Canada,
Mexico, and Australia." I tried to hold in my excitement, but

I asked him how much money he would budget for a project like that. He said that he would like to have it completed for less than six figures.

I told him that I would evaluate the logistics and time involved and get back to him in a couple of days. I left Daisytek that day on cloud nine.

After one meeting, my enthusiasm, passion, and confidence were restored.

Two days later, I returned to Mark's office with my proposal. Since Australia was a logistical challenge, I recommended that we begin with Dallas, Toronto, and Mexico City. After evaluating the requirements, I proposed that the training would be over a six-month period and the cost would be $66,000, plus expenses.

He signed the proposal and I walked out of his office with a check in the amount of $22,000.

I went home that day and I remember vividly where I was when I showed Karen that check. We were both thrilled and thankful. That contract would sustain my business long enough to gather traction to move forward. In fact, over the course of the following 12 months, the training expanded into several other areas of Daisytek. The actual billing exceeded the original proposal by threefold.

Divine intervention? You can think what you want, but I am convinced that God connected Mark and me together for a reason. If I had created a list of 100 people that I thought would be the person to have that kind of impact on my life and business, Mark Layton may not have made my list.

The story did not end there.

Several weeks after I began working with Mark's team, I received a call from someone named Kim from Phoenix. I had no idea who she was but promptly returned her call. Almost immediately into the conversation she said that she believed that I was the answer to her prayers. Surprised by her comment, I asked why. She told me that she was Mark Layton's sister and that she had been praying for years that a Christian man would come along and provide a positive influence for Mark. She was convinced that I was that man.

Who could have put that plan together? Certainly not me.

By the way, a year or so later, CornerStone published the book that Mark provided his feedback on when it was in manuscript form. It was titled *Leadership … Biblically Speaking*. The Chicago story was never printed in the book.

Looking Up

Thanks to the divine intervention of Mark Layton's timing, my business stabilized. I had consistent revenue coming in and, at the same time, I was able to expand my business beyond Daisytek.

Karen was teaching school full time. She was an excellent teacher and was having a positive influence on her students and her peers. On Sundays, she and I enjoyed leading a Bible study class at church. We were a good team.

Jennifer was attending the Dallas Art Institute. Kim was getting ready to attend Texas A&M University. Michael was a junior high student.

We were the All-American family, but our lives were about to change.

Your Grace of Perseverance Applied

It is easy to say that if you persevere long enough, you will succeed. That is what happened to me and, in many cases, that is the truth.

However, if you read this chapter closely, my business partners had to let go. I was the only one who was able to continue. If all three of us had persevered, we would have probably failed together.

Many people give up too soon. They get close to winning and then drop out of the race. However, hanging in there too long could lead to failure, as well.

It is similar to hanging onto a rope. If you are rappelling a mountain, you have to hang onto the rope with all the strength you can muster. Letting go would be catastrophic. If you are water skiing, lose your balance, and are being thrown all over the place, the water will beat you to death if you don't let go of the rope.

The question is, "How do you know whether to hang on or let go?"

I believe that your answer should contain an equal dose of faith and reason. Here is a start. Answer these questions:

1. How do you think that God is directing your life? Are you getting closer to or further away from the person you want to be?

2. Are there enough signs to keep going, or is it just a dream that is not based on solid reasoning?

3. What do your trusted advisers and counselors say? You may only want to listen to yourself, but you will likely only hear what you want to hear. Your answer will be clearer if you involve others.

In my experience, close friends do not make great counselors. They want you to succeed and follow your dream. They don't want to hurt your feelings. Most of the time, they do not have enough experience in the area to provide good advice anyway.

I have found that the best advisers are casual acquaintances – folks who have more experience than you do and who will tell you the truth from their perspectives, even if it hurts your feelings.

My business mentor was the late Fred Smith, Sr., a businessman who lived in Dallas. (He was not related to FedEx's Fred Smith.) We did not know each other until a friend recommended that I call him. We hit it off, but to say that Mr. Smith was brutally honest is an understatement. I will forever be grateful for the wisdom and bold opinions that he provided me during a two-year period to help me discern the path I needed to follow.

If you have diligently prayed, sought wise counsel, and the answer is to stay the course, go all-in. If the answer from your prayers and wise counsel is to pause, or let go of the dream, have the courage to wait or let it go and accept your new path.

eleven

Grace of Suffering

The 'C' Word

The unthinkable happened. Please, God, don't forsake us.

In mid-August 2000, Karen, Kim, Michael, and I loaded all of Kim's personal items into our SUV and headed to College Station, Texas, where Kim was enrolled for her first semester at Texas A&M. We were excited and proud of her. She had been a good student and we knew that she would do well in college and away from home. Regardless, it was still an emotional, traumatic event driving away from College Station without Kim. During the ride home, neither Karen, Michael nor I could speak. All you could hear in our car for three hours was an occasional sniffle from the back, passenger, or driver's seats.

Life without Kim at home would be quite an adjustment for all of us.

Shortly after returning from College Station, Karen began feeling some discomfort in her right breast. She rationalized that she had hurt herself sometime while we were moving Kim into her dorm.

A couple of days passed and her breast became red and swollen. She made an appointment to see her doctor. The next day, her doctor told her that it was probably an infection and prescribed some antibiotics for her to take for two weeks. If her symptoms didn't change, she was to call back.

The antibiotics did not affect the redness or swelling. When she called her doctor, he sent her to a surgeon for a biopsy. I went with her and the surgeon told us that it was probably an infection. There was a slight chance that it was a rare form of breast cancer but not to worry – that would be highly unusual.

There was no breast cancer in Karen's family history. She had a mammogram three months before and everything was normal. She had taken a test to see what her odds of getting breast cancer were, and the odds were as slim as they could be. Knowing those facts, I did not worry at all. Karen was not feeling quite as confident, but we both prayed that it was just an infection that would heal and we would move on with our lives.

September 12, 2000, was an ordinary day … until it wasn't.

Karen and I were both home when the phone rang. I answered it and the surgeon was on the line. He got right to the point. Any time you hear "cancer," "rare," and "critical" in the same sentence, it is jolting. That is what I heard. That is how I felt.

The biopsy results revealed that it was Inflammatory Breast Cancer (IBC), the rare disease he had told us was a slight possibility. He went on to say that since it was the most aggressive breast cancer, it was critical to move quickly. The doctor said it was a Stage 4 cancer. There are only four stages. He tried to encourage us by telling us there had been a lot of advancement in the treatment of this disease. It was no longer a death sentence, as it had been in the past.

The surgeon told me that he had made an appointment for us with an oncologist for the next day at 10 a.m. He provided the name and address of the oncologist. I was in shock when I hung up the phone. I tried to compose myself before I told Karen.

Karen was sitting in the den. As soon as she could see me walking toward her, she immediately sprung up and walked toward me. She knew that something was wrong.

I told her.

We cried.

I tried to encourage her with the little bit of optimism the surgeon had provided me, but we both knew that our lives had just changed.

Do You Want to Live?

The next day at 10 a.m., we were sitting in the oncologist's office. It was strange. We did not exchange many words, but we were both terrified. We felt like we were in a dream – a nightmare.

The doctor was scheduled to be off work that day, but she came to her office specifically to meet with us. She was serious and direct. She told us about the disease and then asked a piercing question that no one would expect to ever have to answer: "Do you want to live?"

Karen, a healthy 47-year-old until the news from the day before, answered, "Yes. Of course, I want to live." The oncologist told her that she was in for the fight of her life beginning right then.

She explained that the cancer did not show on her recent mammogram because IBC, unlike other breast cancers, does not form into a lump. It is like a rash that grows and spreads quickly. It tends to attack younger women than most other breast cancers. The treatment plan is to begin with chemotherapy to try to contain the disease to one area. The next step is a mastectomy to remove the breast. After that, she would have chemotherapy again. The last step of the treatment plan would be 33 rounds of radiation.

Karen asked the hard question: "What are my chances?" The doctor dodged the question by saying that we should not pay attention to statistics. Karen asked again. This time we were told the average lifespan from diagnosis was five years. The first year is the most critical and there was a 50 percent survival rate during the first year. The doctor then attempted to be more encouraging by saying the same thing the surgeon had said the day before … advancements had been made in the treatment of IBC and it was no longer a death sentence. She said that Karen had addressed her situation as soon as she could and that worked to her advantage.

The oncologist then asked us to wait while she made a call to Methodist Hospital. Her office building was connected to the hospital, and when she hung up the phone, she said, "Let's go." She personally walked with us to the surgery area. They were waiting for us and immediately put a hospital gown on Karen. The surgeon on duty then installed a port just below Karen's collarbone for her to receive chemotherapy.

The following day, Thursday, September 14, Karen and I arrived at the treatment room for her first chemotherapy treatment. When we walked into that room, we saw 10 or 12 people, all of them bald, hooked up to IVs. It was shocking. It was surreal. This could not be happening to us. Within the next few minutes, Karen was sitting in what would become a familiar chair with the IV of chemotherapy flowing into her port.

Most people have an adverse physical reaction to chemo, especially in those days. The doctor told us that she probably would not become nauseated for 24 hours. Our best friends, Louis and Stephanie Kruger, came over to be with us that night. No one knew what to do or say.

Louis suggested that we go for a ride and Stephanie would stay with Karen. We left them at home, but we had nowhere to go. We drove around aimlessly. Louis is the only person in the world to whom I could express how I was feeling. He would not judge or respond with a shallow "Oh, it will be all right" comment. Somehow we wound up in a Pep Boys auto supply store. I bought a hydraulic jack. I don't know why I bought it … it was never opened.

When Louis and I returned home, I heard Karen heaving in the master bathroom. When I walked in, I saw Stephanie holding Karen's hair. I will never forget that sight. The chemo had already taken effect in Karen's body.

Her fight had begun.

Kim was scheduled to come home for her first visit from college the next day. We decided to wait until she arrived before telling her the news. Jennifer was living in an apartment in Dallas and she handled the news in her own way. Michael was devastated. He and his mom were extremely close. I was in a reactionary mode clearing my calendar for upcoming chemo treatments and communicating with friends and family.

The next day, Kim and her best friend, Candice, drove home from College Station. As soon as they reached our street, you could hear their car horn honking. They were excited to be coming home for the weekend.

Karen was in her gown and bathrobe. We went to the street to greet the girls. It took Kim about a nanosecond to realize something was not right. Her mom never wore a robe in early evening. When Kim leaped at her to hug, Karen did what she could to protect her port. We moved inside and we told Kim about the situation.

Kim was hysterical. She said that she would stay with her mom and not go back to school. As the weekend progressed, Karen was adamant that Kim would return to school and try to live a normal college life. She said that only she could fight this fight and the best thing Kim could do for her mom was to go back to school. She promised that if anything unexpected happened, she would call her immediately.

On Sunday, Kim returned to school at A&M. Many of her Aggie friends knew and loved Karen. They provided Kim a great support team while we were all trying to deal with our new reality.

Getting in Fighting Shape

A fellow chemo patient told Karen that losing your hair is emotionally draining. She said that if you see your hair coming out as you shampoo every day, you go through emotional trauma every day. Her suggestion was to be proactive and buy a wig before your hair begins to fall out. When it does begin to fall out, cut it all off at one time. We took her advice.

One of Karen's best physical features had always been her hair. Everywhere she went, people commented on its color and fullness. Losing her hair was not going to be easy and it would affect her self-esteem. Finding the perfect wig was important. We looked at several wig shops in Dallas without luck. She was getting discouraged. She finally found the right wig in Waxahachie, a town just south of Dallas.

It wasn't long before her hair began falling out. The advice we received was right … it was traumatic and discouraging to see patches of her beautiful hair lying on the shower floor.

I bought a barber's clipper-and-trimmer set so we could buzz her hair. Karen sat in the bathtub and Michael and I shaved her head. We tried to make it as pleasant as we could, but it was not real pleasant. She got out of the tub, put on her wig and said, "I don't look that bad."

Michael and a couple of his friends shaved their heads in support of his mom.

Our entire family was getting in fighting shape. The chemo treatment cycle was once a week for two months. Karen did not want to go on disability. She wanted to continue to teach school, which was against my wishes. Her oncologist encouraged her to keep working if she could. The doctor said that it would be good for her to keep her life as normal as possible. I disagreed. Looking back, it kept her mind occupied and she was inspired by the kids in her class. It probably was the best course of action for her.

Her new schedule was to receive chemo on Friday, recover through the weekend, and show up at work on Monday. The teachers in her pod volunteered to write her lesson plans. Other teachers at the school would grade her students' papers.

Karen's fourth-graders were learning a lot more about life than your typical fourth-grader. Each of her students wrote her a letter of encouragement. The following is an example of one of her student's thoughts:

> *Mrs. Cottrell, I love you very much and I hope you come back. You got ever body worried about you and I really hope you come back cause if you don't I am going to cry my heart off. Ms. Maffiey was already crying and others was to. I really hope you get this message and if you don't that is all right cause if you die, I will put this in that box you are going to be in and I am goint to be at your funnerl too if my mom drive me there. I hope you come back to school Monday. I love you very very very very much and don't forget that Mrs. Cottrell.*
> *— Jammie*

Karen loved reading the students' letters. Regardless of how their love was expressed, she knew that they were sincere. It lifted her spirits.

Get to the Hospital Right Now

We got into our treatment groove. Karen was doing reasonably well until we had a life-threatening scare. It was on a Friday night. We had a Friday night family tradition of going to Florisitas, a local Mexican restaurant. That evening Karen said that she was too tired and did not want to go. Michael and I left her resting on the sofa while we went to eat.

When we returned an hour or so later, she was burning up. Her fever was over 105. I called the oncologist and she said to go to the hospital immediately. She would call the emergency room and tell them that we were on our way.

We lived only five minutes from the hospital. When we arrived, they were waiting on us and immediately took her to a room. There were two life-threatening dangers involved. First, while on chemo you have very little resistance to infection. If you are around anyone sick, you are in danger. That is why they took Karen immediately to a room instead of having her wait in the emergency room. Second, if her port had become infected, she would develop a staph infection directly into her bloodstream. That is what had happened. We did not know at the time the danger of the situation. By the grace of God, she was cared for quickly and was able to go home a few days later.

Karen went on to complete chemotherapy, the first part of her treatment plan. Amazingly, she stuck to her original plan and taught school while fighting through her chemo treatments.

Next Up, Mastectomy

The next stage of treatment was to have a radical mastectomy. She scheduled the mastectomy for November 17, the week before Thanksgiving, so that she would have the Thanksgiving and Christmas breaks to recover.

The mastectomy surgery was successful and went as well as it could, but it was an emotional low for all our family. We could see how sick she was and how she had been beaten up by the chemo and mastectomy trauma to her body. The surgeon also removed 16 lymph nodes to determine if the cancer was present throughout her body. The results revealed that nine of the sixteen lymph nodes were positive for cancer.

On Thanksgiving Day, Karen walked from our bedroom to the dining room for Thanksgiving dinner. All of our family were there to celebrate those few steps. That was one of my most proud moments for her.

Donna Berryman, the mother of Kim's friend Candice, was in nursing school. Donna volunteered to come every day to change Karen's dressing on her mastectomy wound. That was supposed to be my job, but I could not do it. I had reconciled that I would take her to the doctor's office every day to have it done. When Donna volunteered to come each day, we accepted that as a tremendous God-send.

The people in our church brought meals to our home for months. We did not have enough room to store the meals in our freezer. Everyone wanted to help, and we were glad to allow them to help in any way they could.

Christmas came and went. Karen was getting stronger every day, and there would be a break for her to recover before her next treatment of another round of chemotherapy. She returned to teaching her fourth-graders when school began after the Christmas break.

Everyone was encouraged by her progress. Yet we knew that she was still in the early stages of the fight of her life.

A Different Blow

Karen had been gaining strength every day. The side effects of the chemotherapy were easing off and she was recovering well from her mastectomy.

CornerStone was staying afloat. Every month we were putting money away for future book investments. Daisytek had provided steady income, and I was able to be with Karen for every appointment that I needed to be. Things seemed to be stabilizing, although the thought of the next round of chemotherapy was never far from our minds.

On April 11, my father passed away from a heart attack. It was another shock for our family. He was 79 and in good health. He played golf two days before his heart attack.

I was especially close to my dad and was having a hard time reconciling why these tragedies were happening.

After my father's death, I thought that I should get a checkup to make sure my health was holding up under the personal and professional stress that I had been experiencing for the last few years. Dad's death scared me because heart disease was prevalent in our family. My sister Evelyn had pericarditis, an inflammation of the lining of the heart, in 1978. My dad had a triple bypass in 1979. My sister Sherry had a quadruple bypass in 1994. My mom had a triple bypass in 1997. The deck was stacked with odds that I would probably have a heart event sometime in my life.

I went to my family doctor for a checkup. I was 47 years old, felt fine, was reasonably active, and not overweight. My blood work and EKG were normal. Because of my family history, my doctor recommended I go to a cardiologist for a stress test.

I made an appointment and went to the cardiologist. I had never experienced any heart problem symptoms except high cholesterol, which had been controlled by medicine. There was no need to load Karen up with another potential worry, so I did not tell her about my appointment. During my stress test, I walked more than 10 minutes before my heart rate got to my target rate. The test was no problem. However, the cardiologist said that he wanted me to come back the next day for a nuclear imaging test called a thallium stress test. I was not overly alarmed and returned the next day for the more extensive test.

Again, the exercise portion of the thallium stress test was no problem for me.

The following day, the cardiologist called. He said that my stress test results showed that I had early stages of blockage. I would need an arteriogram to determine exactly how extensive the blockage was. He said that Baylor Hospital in Dallas had the capability to perform an angioplasty, if needed, while I was having the arteriogram.

I was scheduled to be in Cleveland, ironically at the Cleveland Clinic, to facilitate a leadership seminar the following Wednesday. The cardiologist said that the angioplasty and arteriogram were not major surgery. He added that if I had the procedure on Friday, I would be fine by Monday. He also said that I would be able to fly to Cleveland on Tuesday – no problem. That was the plan.

I arrived at Baylor Hospital early Friday morning. By that time, I had told Karen the situation, and Michael, Kimberly, and Evelyn went with Karen and me to the hospital. Shortly after we arrived, I was on a gurney headed to get my arteriogram and angioplasty, if it was needed.

I was given a mild sedative and was semi-awake when they injected the dye through a catheter. I could see several monitors and screens on my left and the doctor and nurse were on my right side. I could not figure out anything on the screens, but I could hear the doctor speaking. He was talking to the nurse and said, "We are not going to be able to do this one." I was the only other person in the room. I remember wondering what he was talking about.

It wasn't long before I knew what he was talking about. He told me that I had four clogged arteries. Three were 90 percent closed and one was 70 percent closed. The angioplasty would not work for me. I would have to have quadruple bypass heart surgery.

Boom. The news made me angry. I had already had enough of tests, hospitals, doctors, and medicine. This was not fair.

The doctor went to the waiting room to tell my family. Karen, who was bald from chemo and still recovering from her mastectomy, became hysterical. Kim and Michael were shocked and crying. Evelyn had her hands full trying to calm everyone. It was not one of our best days.

Get Your Affairs Together

The doctor admitted me to the hospital that day. They would work my surgery in on Monday, June 11, 2001. That happened to be two months to the day after my father passed. His death probably saved my life. I had no symptoms and would not have gone in for a checkup if his death had not scared me.

The weekend before my heart surgery was a fog. The doctor told me to get my affairs together. There was a 3 percent mortality rate for this surgery. Three percent doesn't sound too daunting unless you are the person they are talking about. My affairs were in good shape, so we did not have to scramble for any paperwork or attorneys. The last thing we needed at that time was for an attorney to show up.

Kim had been dating a guy from A&M named Huntleigh Harris. He was coming up from College Station to be with her. Karen and I had never met him, but Kim wanted him there. When he arrived, Karen was bald and sitting beside my bed. I was in the bed and they had just shaved me from neck to toe. Meeting his girlfriend's parents in the conditions that we were in had to be a shock for Huntleigh. He had to be wondering how fast he could get back to College Station. If he were to marry into this family, what would he be getting into? He must have really loved Kim, because he handled the situation well. He stayed the entire weekend to help Kim.

A few years later, Karen and I were toasting Kim and Huntleigh at their wedding.

During the late afternoon of June 11, my surgeon, Dr. Thomas Hoang, told me that it was almost time for surgery. He said that there was a new procedure to use the radial artery from my arm instead of a vein from my leg for my bypass. That would be in addition to the internal mammary artery. The radial artery should be stronger and possibly last longer than a vein from my leg. I asked if it would impact my golf game. He was a golfer and guaranteed me that it would not. I gave the okay to take the radial artery, and it has lasted more than 17 years so far.

The surgery went well. I had no problems with my arm or my chest where they cracked it open. My recovery was rapid. I went home on Friday, June 15.

What's This Knot?

My heart follow-up appointments were good. The only issue I had was a knot on the side of my neck. I knew that the IV was inserted close to where that knot had appeared. Dr. Hoang said that the knot did not have anything to do with my heart surgery.

I went to a neck and throat specialist. He felt the hard knot. He said that it was probably an infection … words that I had heard before. After a week of antibiotics, the knot was still there. He said it could be cancer and that I needed to have surgery to take the knot out. Another surgery, another could-be cancer, more hospitals, doctors, and medicine.

Lying in bed the night before the neck surgery, I remember praying, "I know you promised that you would not give me more than I can handle, but I am tapped out. Please let this knot go away and allow me to go on living."

I was at the end of my rope.

Neck surgery is dicey. There are a lot of things that can go wrong if the surgeon makes a mistake. Fortunately, he didn't. The surgeon discovered my knot was an encapsulated infection. He removed it and I never had any more issues with my neck.

Back to the Fight

Karen had beaten the 50/50 odds that she would live a year. She had survived chemo and her mastectomy. Now it was time for more chemo.

Karen's previous experience with chemo helped as she prepared for a second round. I guess that when you have been through chemo once, some of the fear is diminished. She knew what to expect, the environment was familiar, and she knew that she could make it.

We both also knew how tough it was. I wanted her to quit teaching. She said, "no." I told her that if she was going to continue teaching, maybe she should teach at Ovilla Christian School, a small school where Michael was a sophomore. I thought the environment at Ovilla would be much easier and less stressful on her. She did not want to leave the Duncanville Independent School District. She said, "They need me more there." That was that. She would teach another year.

She began chemo again. Her response to the treatments was good. She would have treatment on Friday, be sick on Saturday, recover on Sunday, and go to school Monday. She was a strong and determined woman. We worked it out where she would have chemo while I was in rehab for my heart. She completed her chemo after a couple of months.

On to Radiation
Karen's mastectomy had healed well, largely because of the good care of Donna Berryman. A few months after her second chemo series, it was time to begin radiation. Thirty-three treatments were scheduled.

On the first visit to the radiation oncologist, they permanently marked on her chest where the radiation was to be administered. The markings were called "reference points" and were similar to a tattoo. Those reference points would be the guide for the oncologist to deliver the radiation to the exact right place every time. The doctor warned Karen before her first treatment that by the end of the treatments she would not want to come see him.

It wasn't long before we knew what he meant.

Karen would go to radiation every day after school.

Administering radiation did not take very long, and after the first treatment, there was no pain. It was a piece of cake after all she had been through. The next few treatments were not bad, either. However, after about 10 treatments, it was not a piece of cake any longer. The radiation was essentially burning her burn. You can imagine how painful that was even for just a couple of minutes. By the end of the treatments, it was torture.

Great Celebration

Finally, it was time for the last radiation treatment. She had fought the fight of her life through chemo, mastectomy, chemo again, and radiation. She had beaten all the odds.

It was a Friday afternoon when she finished her last radiation treatment. She was exhausted and emotionally drained. As soon as we got home, she said that she wanted to go to bed. I told her it was time to celebrate. Michael and I convinced her that we needed to go to Florisitas, our Friday night restaurant. She pushed back but finally said okay.

One of the most enjoyable meals of my life was that night. Michael and I walked her into Florisitas, arm in arm. When we entered through the door, already sitting in the restaurant and waiting on us were 30 of her best friends. Twenty-nine women from school, church, and our neighborhood, plus one man whom she worked with. The staff at Florisitas had decorated the restaurant for her without me knowing it. They joined in our celebration.

Every person at that dinner had prayed for Karen for a long, long time. They had completed her lesson plans, graded her papers, substituted in her class, and brought to our home meal after meal. We had a prayer of thanksgiving together.

It was a great celebration.

The treatments had taken about three years. The notes of congratulations from her fourth-grade students were proof that she had made a positive difference in their lives.

Karen was content and happy. She wanted to live, and she had fought the fight.

After her treatments were completed, her cancer was in remission. She lived a cancer-free life for seven years. We traveled all over the world together and enjoyed our gift of life.

Your Grace of Suffering Applied

I struggled writing this chapter. You may question how each of the events – cancer, chemo, mastectomy, radiation, my father's death, and my heart surgery – could be grace.

Me too.

Is there grace in suffering? How can our most vulnerable and challenging moments of suffering be grace?

I can't answer those questions. I don't know all of the lives that were touched by Karen's cancer journey. I don't know what happened to Karen's peers, who watched her faith grow instead of wither during her suffering. I don't know what happened to those fourth-graders who saw that Karen loved them so much that she wanted to be with them during her time of suffering. I don't know if I would still be alive if my dad had not had a fatal heart attack.

There are a lot of things that I don't know, and will probably never know, while I am taking breaths on this earth.

But, there are some things that I do know:

I know that God was always with us.

I know that our faith was strengthened by our suffering.

I know that God is faithful regardless of how well I understand my sufferings.

I know that God uses our tragedy as well as our triumphs for His glory and our ultimate good.

My conclusion is that I must depend on the fact that God's definition of grace is probably completely different from my definition of grace. I can't comprehend … and I will never be able to comprehend … how He uses the suffering in my life for His glory.

However, one of the most powerful and wonderful gifts I have been given is the gift of hope. Everything in this life and our next life hinges on the grace of hope. When I have hope, I can move forward. Without hope, there is no reason to keep moving.

In John 14, Jesus said, *"Do not let your hearts be troubled. You believe in God, believe also in me. My Father's house has many rooms; if that were not so, would I have told you that I am going there to prepare a place for you? And if I go and prepare a place for you, I will come back and take you to be with me that you also may be where I am. You know the way to the place where I am going."*

Keeping my heart from being troubled is easy when things are good. Actually, the only time my heart would ever be troubled would be during my times of crisis, suffering, anxiety, and fear. Jesus was talking directly to me in my most vulnerable time. He promised me that I have hope in something that is far greater than anything I can comprehend.

It is up to me to believe that His promise is true, and I have to trust in the One who made it.

I don't know why all of those events took place in our lives. You may have things happen in your life that you will never be able to comprehend, either. Regardless of how much you understand your own suffering, I encourage you to never lose hope and embrace the promises of the One who gives us our eternal hope.

twelve

Mind-blowing Grace

Monday Morning Leadership

Monday morning, it was all I hoped it would be.
— "Monday Monday," THE MAMAS & THE PAPAS

While Karen and I were focused on our medical challenges, my business continued to do reasonably well. I was able to pay the bills and create more products even while waiting in the chemo room with Karen or completing my heart rehabilitation.

Shortly after Karen's final radiation treatment, I experienced divine intervention again in the form of a book titled *Monday Morning Leadership*.

Before I write about the backstory of *Monday Morning*, it is important to understand how unique that book is compared to the normal cycle of creating and producing a book.

- ✦ *Monday Morning* took days to visualize the concepts in the book instead of weeks.

- ✦ It took two days to write the first complete draft instead of months.

✦ Final edits took a couple of weeks instead of volleying the manuscript back and forth between the editors and me for a couple of months.

✦ It has been a perennial best-seller for 16 years.

For these unique events to happen, I am convinced that, for whatever reason, *Monday Morning Leadership* was God's special gift to me.

Here is the backstory. In 2002, I was on a business trip from Dallas to Atlanta. During the plane ride, I read a book titled *Tuesdays With Morrie* by Mitch Albom. The book was a compelling story about Mitch, a former student at Brandeis University, and his college professor, Morrie Schwartz. Near the end of the professor's life, Morrie and Mitch agreed to meet every Tuesday for Morrie to share thoughts and experiences. I found the book to be interesting as Morrie taught Mitch stories weekly about his life. The wisdom shared by the professor was insightful, although not real inspirational. I enjoyed the book, but I finished it feeling more depressed than when I started.

The following week I was traveling to Toronto to conduct a leadership session for Daisytek. While on the trip, I began thinking: Why not write an inspirational *Tuesdays with Morrie*-type book that would teach business principles? The book could be about a trusted mentor who guides a young leader whose career may have hit a snag. The book would contain practical lessons that would also provide tools, hope, and inspiration to the reader.

The thought would not leave me, but my more prevalent and realistic thought was, "I am not sure how to put that together in a business book."

The Toronto trip was during the days when traveling on Saturday would reduce your airfare by about half. Mark Layton and I had agreed for me to travel on weekends to save on Daisytek's expenses. So, I was alone on a Saturday night in a hotel room in a Toronto suburb, scribbling notes about my thoughts on *Tuesdays With Morrie*. Suddenly, out of the blue, my book became crystal clear. The book would be fictional. It would be based on my experiences and observations. It would address issues that every manager faces. The mentor's wisdom would encourage and guide the manager through crisis situations. For several weeks, the fictional characters would meet on Mondays.

At that time, and even today, common challenges that all managers face were obvious: accepting responsibility without excuses, maintaining focus, staying connected with the team, maintaining integrity, making great hires and coaching, managing time, providing recognition, and seeking continuous improvement. I narrowed my list down to those eight areas. I wanted the book to be brief so that people would actually take the time to read it. Those eight challenges became stand-alone chapter ideas to form the outline of the book.

I have read and heard how people have had an "out of body" experience, an unexpected touch, or a feeling that their experiences and talents were used by God in a miraculous way. I took those stories with a grain of salt until it happened to me with *Monday Morning*.

Providential Writing

I did not write *Monday Morning Leadership*. Oh, my hands were on the keyboard, but the inspiration came from a power greater than me. Ideas and words started to flow like never

before or since. For two days, my experiences at Xerox, FedEx, NSG, and CornerStone were interwoven securely together to create one seamless story.

The characters quickly revealed themselves as people whom I knew. The main character was the mentor, Tony Pearce, who was named after Tony Van Roekel – the person who promoted me into my first leadership position at Xerox – and Pearce, my father-in-law. The struggling manager was Jeff Walters (the combined names of two different guys whom I was mentoring at the time). The remainder of the characters were named after family members: Karen, Michael, Kim, Jeni, and several other friends.

I could not sleep. The keyboard was sizzling.

The chapter on accepting responsibility became Drivers and Passengers, which was initiated from a casual conversation with my friend Louis Krueger.

Focus became Keep the Main Thing the Main Thing based on direction given by Jim Barksdale with FedEx.

Staying connected with the team became Escape From Management Land based on a brief conversation with Dan Amos, CEO of Aflac.

The integrity chapter became The Do Right Rule based on my father's teachings to me.

Hiring and coaching became Hire Tough based on a conversation with my friend Eric Harvey.

Time management evolved into Do Less or Work Faster based on my previous booklet, *175 Ways to Get More Done in Less Time.*

Recognition became Buckets and Dippers based on a private conversation with the late Don Clifton.

Continuous improvement evolved into Enter the Learning Zone based on a private conversation with Zig Ziglar.

Tuesday evening when I returned home to Dallas, the book was complete. Done. A normal book-writing process usually takes several months to complete the first draft. *Monday Morning Leadership* was completed in a weekend.

Finding the Right Publisher

There are over 17,000 business books printed each year. That number does not include self-published or digital books. Looking at *Monday Morning Leadership* through my lens, it was obvious that every business book publisher would want the honor of bidding to publish my new title. I prayed that God would give me wisdom to discern how to choose the best publisher for this project. It was extremely important to line up with the right publisher, because I knew this book was going to be a hit.

My agent, David Hale-Smith, presented the manuscript to every major business book publisher. No one was interested. Not one publishing house made an offer. I could not believe it. There are tons of publishers, and every door was shut. Even Walk The Talk's Eric Harvey, publisher of several of my booklets, turned down *Monday Morning Leadership*.

I was incredibly disappointed.

The only avenue remaining was for CornerStone to publish the book … an expensive and risky route at that time.

CornerStone had been publishing business booklets for a couple of years. We had success when we published *Becoming the Obvious Choice, 175 Ways to Get More Done in Less Time, Listen Up, Teacher!,* and *136 Effective Presentation Tips.*

I studied and understood the direct-mail and publishing market. I knew how to publish and market booklets, but *Monday Morning Leadership* was different. It was a 112-page book, not a 56-page booklet. It addressed a broad topic of leadership instead of providing solutions to specific problems.

This book was a different animal. Instead of a false cover, the book would require an envelope. Due to size and weight, the printing and mailing cost of *Monday Morning Leadership* was significantly more than the cost of the booklets. The risk was more than I was comfortable with. Even with dozens of rejections, I did not lose confidence in the content.

God did answer my prayer, but the answer was not on my list of potential publishers. Without any other viable options, I decided to take the risk and and let CornerStone publish *Monday Morning Leadership.*

That decision changed my life.

Our first print run was 22,000 books. The last week of December 2002, my direct-mail-campaign company delivered 15,165 *Monday Morning Leadership* books to the post office. The books were mailed to my customer base and to names that had a good purchase rate of my previous booklets.

That mail drop kept me awake for a few nights. What if they never left the mail station? What if they were damaged in the mail? What if no one bought a book? There was a plethora of things to worry about. It cost about $25,000 for this experiment. The retail price of the book was $12.95. So, we needed to sell a bunch of books.

By this time, CornerStone had just two employees, my neighbor, Barbara Bartlett, and me. When my office lease expired, Jennifer's former bedroom became my office.

I think it's safe to say that CornerStone was on the cutting edge of remote offices … by necessity. Our 800-number calls went to Barbara's home. Our customers probably thought we were a bigger, more successful company than we were. Books were stored in a warehouse close to my home. Every day I took a load of books to Barbara for her to pack and ship.

In mid-January 2003, orders for *Monday Morning Leadership* began to come in. We sold 4,609 books in that first month, generating over $50,000 in revenue. And, we still had books remaining in inventory to be sold.

Holy cow! I submitted a purchase order to print 50,000 more books. My printer was in Peoria, Illinois, and they were wondering what was going on. Thankfully, my credit was good.

The orders for books continued to climb. In February, we mailed 15,000. In March, we sent out another 18,000. In June, we mailed 27,000 more books. We could not print and mail the books fast enough. The more we gave away, the more we sold. I was spending every evening manually recording all of our sales activity and maintaining our customer-base intelligence.

Barbara was on the phone all day taking orders. Her evenings were spent fulfilling the orders. It was great, but we could not continue at that pace.

We raised the price of *Monday Morning Leadership* to $14.95. It did not affect the order rate. That move was unheard of in the traditional book-selling model. In fact, everything about *Monday Morning* was contrary to the conventional retail book-selling theories.

The successful *Monday Morning Leadership* launch was propelled by a couple of unrelated significant events.

Amazon

The internet was in its infancy and was growing at an astronomical rate. Customers were beginning to adapt to the idea of buying certain products online. Selling books online fit the emerging trend perfectly. There was a small company in Seattle leading the movement. The company was Amazon. Their only service at that time was selling books and music on compact discs. I contacted Amazon and became one of their first small-publisher customers.

Shortly after becoming an Amazon vendor, I was in Seattle for a business meeting. I asked my contact at Amazon if I could come by and see their facility. He told me that they did not have anything to show. They were working out of a warehouse.

Even while working out of a warehouse, they had a creative online marketing system. They were progressive in suggestive selling. When someone bought a book on leadership, they suggested to the customer that they might want to consider *Monday Morning Leadership*. It was brilliant. Because of Amazon, customers living all over the world were exposed to my products when they purchased leadership books by other authors.

Amazon used technology to do the same things traditional retailers were doing, except it was electronic and better. In the retail environment, all business books are sorted together on a shelf. Even the largest retailers have only 20 or so leadership books on the shelf at any one time. Amazon could electronically feature hundreds of books on their "shelves" as opposed to the few on the retailers' shelves. They created the search inside the book feature where a shopper could "flip through the pages" of a book before buying. Amazon made it easy to search, to browse, and to buy books 24/7 without leaving your home or office. In addition, readers would provide instant feedback through reviews and ratings. Instant customer feedback had never been available before.

It was brilliant marketing.

The traditional publishing system was antiquated. There was a loop, beginning with large publishers printing and providing books to wholesalers so they could deliver the books to distributors, who lastly got the books to retailers. Retailers were left to wait for customers to walk in their store to buy a book. That was a lot of movements, each one with an open hand in the pie. And, the author was still responsible for driving people into the retail store.

On the financial side, retailing books the traditional way allowed authors to receive a small royalty. A retailer would feature a book on his shelf for a short time period. Soon another new book would become the latest, greatest flavor. A book would either be sold or returned to the publisher within six months. The author would receive a royalty statement nine months after the book was published and every six months thereafter.

Amazon's system provided instant information instead of nine-month-old information. Amazon paid a significantly higher royalty each month rather than every six months. Their system provided daily information on the number of book sales. I could see exactly what my check would be at the end of the month. They had literally built a better mousetrap using the new world of automation and the internet.

Without Amazon's platform, it would have been impossible for me to market my products all over the world. Amazon leveled the field with the large publishing houses. Small publishers like CornerStone had the prospect of selling more books than at any other time in history. Thank you, Amazon.

CornerStone Automation and Fulfillment

About that same time, I met Lee Colan, who became one of my most trusted business partners. In a client's office, Lee saw a box of *Becoming the Obvious Choice* booklets. Lee is a smart guy and thought that he could produce a rapid-read product like that booklet.

Lee called and we met so that I could describe what I was doing. We worked a deal where I would publish his booklets and he could use my "system." That was a good business decision for both of us and continues to this day.

During the meeting, I shared with Lee that I needed to automate our processes. My business was outrunning our capabilities. Lee suggested that I talk to Harry Hopkins, a young IT guru. Harry had recently completed a business automation project for Lee.

I called Harry and scheduled a meeting at a Dallas restaurant. Harry walked in unshaven, donning long hair, and carrying a motorcycle helmet under his arm. He didn't even bring a notepad. I was the typical conservative corporate type. Lee had not warned me about Harry's youth and appearance. After talking to Harry for a few minutes, I knew that he was smart, listened well, and could create a better system for me than I could conceive for myself. We made a deal and he began to automate my order taking, fulfillment, mail lists, and everything else. He was amazing.

In the meantime, as my system was being developed, business was booming. I attempted to move the fulfillment role to a local mail shop, but that did not work. I later moved it to my mail distribution company, but that did not work well, either.

MultiAd was the company in Peoria, Illinois, printing CornerStone's books. Jim Garner worked for MultiAd. I received a call from Jim informing me that MultiAd would soon begin a distribution division. Jim proposed that I allow MultiAd to provide fulfillment, along with printing needs for CornerStone. MultiAd had become a wonderful partner. I trusted their leaders, yet having all of my products 700 miles away was a new and uncomfortable concept to me.

Because of the work that Harry was doing for us in automation, moving everything to Peoria was a possibility. It would also save me the cost of shipping books to a Dallas warehouse.

Moving fulfillment to Illinois would mean that I had all my eggs in MultiAd's basket. I flew to Peoria to see exactly what they had in mind and to hear directly from the owners what they were proposing. After spending time with the MultiAd team, I was convinced that they could solve all of my distribution problems. They did.

The More You Sell, the More You Sell

At the same time *Monday Morning Leadership* began to sell, customers were calling to inquire about me speaking at their management and leadership conferences. I limited myself to 26 appearances a year and my calendar was full.

I could not be everywhere, so I created a *Monday Morning* Training Kit. It consisted of a facilitator guide, participant guide, audio tape, two coffee mugs, and a PowerPoint presentation all packaged in a really nice-looking kit. Clients could use the material to train their own team. I remember thinking the kit would be a large expense and high risk for me. I would have to sell 60 kits to break even. I was not sure that was feasible, but I did it anyway.

We sold more than 500 of those kits the first year.

A lot was happening at one time and it was difficult for Barbara and me to keep up with everything. We expanded our team to include Michele Lucia as my business manager to handle the speaking portion of the business. Suzanne McClelland began working with Barbara in customer service. Harry was my automation guru. Melissa Farr was my graphic designer. Jack Bartlett was my accountant. They are still on my team 17 years later.

Eventually, Ken Carnes returned to CornerStone and created a new entity, CornerStone Services, which would be the consulting and coaching arm for our customers. He created a nice business around *Monday Morning Leadership*.

When *Monday Morning* had sold over 200,000 copies and was recognized as a top 15 business book in *BusinessWeek* magazine, all the major publishers were suddenly interested in the rights to the book. At that point, there was no way that I would give up the rights to *Monday Morning Leadership* to another publisher.

HarperCollins proposed that we add a couple of chapters, beef up the content in some of the other chapters, and allow them to publish a new, enhanced hardcover version of *Monday Morning Leadership* to be titled *Monday Morning Mentoring*. I would keep *Monday Morning Leadership* and continue doing what I was doing through CornerStone.

That was a good deal for HarperCollins and me. They paid me a nice advance and *Monday Morning Mentoring* became a best-selling book for them. Shortly therafter, we completed a contract for them to publish two other CornerStone products under a different title: *Monday Morning Choices* (originally published as *12 Choices … That Lead to Your Success*) and *Monday Morning Motivation* (originally published as *Leadership Energy*).

Once our CornerStone system was in place, it was easy to expand products. Lee Colan had developed an impressive array of business booklets. Together, he and I provided a steady stream of new products for CornerStone. He became one of my closest business advisers and we co-authored a beautiful coffee-table-size picture book titled *The Nature of Excellence*. The spectacular photographs in the book were taken by Tom Fox. That was one of my most enjoyable projects. I also was publishing books for other authors in a joint venture.

Several of my books were picked up by major publishers after CornerStone had published an earlier version. In addition to the HarperCollins Monday Morning series, *The Magic Question, Indispensable, Tuesday Morning Coaching,* and *The*

First Two Rules of Leadership were all published in a soft cover by CornerStone before the major publishers published their hardcover versions.

Monday Morning Leadership was the engine that drove the CornerStone train, and it still is. The book has sold well over a million copies. It is published in more than a dozen different languages. I have spoken to groups about *Monday Morning Leadership* in 42 states. Karen and I traveled to England, Rio de Janeiro, Panama City, Montreal, Toronto, Hawaii, and several other incredible destinations paid for by organizations that wanted to learn about *Monday Morning Leadership.*

Karen's favorite destination was Stratford-upon-Avon. We thought it was pretty cool that I was asked to speak at William Shakespeare's birthplace.

Reflecting on the sequence of events that led to CornerStone's success, it is beyond belief. Who could plan on Mark Layton, Eric Harvey, Lee Colan, Barbara Bartlett, Harry Hopkins, Jim Garner, and all the rest of the CornerStone team lining up with their unique talents at the right place at the right time for me? No one could.

What if a major publisher had visualized the potential of *Monday Morning Leadership* the same way as I did? Who knows which direction I may have gone. No matter how difficult it was for me to accept the closed doors, in my case for sure, those doors were closed and locked for my own protection.

Monday Morning Leadership combined many of my experiences into one concise, rapid-read book that has influenced many people worldwide. I could not do that. I did not do that.

It was a gift that was given to me that was far greater than anything I would have ever asked.

It was mind-blowing grace.

Your Mind-blowing Grace Applied

Early in this book, I shared with you that during our engagement, Karen and I agreed to always look for a great surprise after a disappointment. We never envisioned that the disappointment would be so devastating as cancer, nor the surprise to be so extraordinary as the success of *Monday Morning Leadership,* but that is what happened to us.

Every leadership consultant on the planet will tell you that your success will ultimately depend upon the people whom you have on your team. Learn from me. I am a great example of that philosophy. The people on my team, the vendors that I worked with, and the customers who bought from us, were all mind-blowing graces. I just tried to run as fast as I could to stay in front of the parade.

I hope that you will begin looking for your great surprise after a disappointment. You will probably be amazed at your own mind-blowing grace.

thirteen

Grace of Fresh Starts

New Beginnings in Horseshoe Bay

We had been through a turbulent time. We needed to reboot.
We chose to start fresh in Horseshoe Bay, Texas.

Karen's cancer had been in remission for two years. Those were good years for us. We were enjoying living a normal, cancer-free life.

A friend of ours, Daryl Kirkham, had a lake house on Lake LBJ in Horseshoe Bay, Texas, a resort community about three hours south of Dallas. Daryl invited us to go down for the weekend to relax and play golf. Karen and I thought that was a good idea. It was a going to be a nice, quick weekend getaway.

The weekend turned into more than just a getaway.

As we drove into Horseshoe Bay, we were stunned at how beautiful it was. God did some really nice work there. It was a golfers' paradise with four championship golf courses. Water enthusiasts loved it because it was on Lake LBJ. This lake is at a constant level lake controlled by dams on each end. Marble

Falls was the nearest town, about 15 minutes away. Austin was the nearest big city, about an hour east. San Antonio was about an hour-and-a-half south.

We loved what we saw, and we wanted to find out more. Daryl provided us with the name of his Realtor, Ted Burgett, who would show us around.

I played golf at one of the Horseshoe Bay courses on Friday. On Saturday morning we hooked up with Ted, a native of the area. Ted was an encyclopedia of information about the Horseshoe Bay real estate market. While giving us a tour, he received a call from his office – a lot had just come on the market. Ted did not know exactly where the lot was and asked Karen and me if we wanted to check it out. We didn't have anything else planned. We said, "Sure, let's go and take a look."

We drove to 205 Apache Tears. South of the lot was a huge, beautiful home. It was the only house within about a half mile. The lot that had just come on the market was heavily wooded, making it difficult to see much of its view. The back of the lot was on the sixth green of the Applerock Golf Course. The lot sloped radically from the road down to the green. I stepped up on top of the neighbor's driveway wall to try to sneak a glance at the view that the lot would have. It was breathtaking. You could see for at least 20 miles. The lake was in view, and it was on the golf course.

I asked Ted if he knew any of the details about the lot. He called his office and learned that it was being sold because of a family issue and they needed to move the lot quickly.

As I mentioned earlier, I am decisive. I was looking for a project that Karen could be involved in to help her move forward and plan our future together. She and I briefly discussed purchasing the lot and agreed to submit an offer. We returned to DeSoto that Sunday. On Monday, Ted called to inform us that the owners of the lot had refused our offer with no counter offer. Ted believed we could get the lot with a little higher offer. We agreed to try again. Ted presented our offer and it was accepted.

All of the sudden we owned a spectacular lot in Horseshoe Bay. Michael was a junior in high school. We had already decided that we would not consider moving until one year after he graduated. Since he knew no one in Horseshoe Bay, we felt it was important for him to have a year to come back to his DeSoto home for visits from college.

Our plan was to build on our lot within a year or so. But, the "let's begin later" plan was contrary to my "let's do it now" mentality.

Karen was still teaching school, but she was about ready to hang up the chalk. I loved the lot we bought and was eager to begin playing regularly on the incredible Horseshoe Bay golf courses. The more I thought about it, the more I was convinced that there was not a good reason to postpone building our new home. We could go ahead and build in Horseshoe Bay and Karen would retire in a year. Our main residence would continue to be in DeSoto. We decided to build the house as soon as possible.

Jen and Kim at Michael's
high school graduation

We now had a firm, positive plan for Karen to work on. That plan lifted her spirits.

Karen enjoyed working with Pete Strobel, our wonderful builder. She designed the downstairs of her dream house. I designed my dream office, conference room, and media room upstairs. Building our home was the perfect project for Karen at that time.

One of my objectives was to build our home and to move into it as stress-free as possible. A few months before completion, Karen, Kim, Kim's friend Candice, and our decorator drove to Austin on a Sunday morning to shop for furniture. I had previously explained Karen's situation to the owner of Louis Shanks Furniture Store. He graciously opened the store solely for us. A store decorator joined Karen and her team to pick out every single piece of furniture for our new house. It was a very expensive day.

Upon completion of the Horseshoe Bay house in the summer of 2005, the new furniture was delivered and placed by the decorators. When Karen and I walked in, it was ready for us to enjoy.

Our home had two large balconies with amazing 20-mile views, and that is where we spent our time. We fell in love with our new home. It was beyond our wildest dreams.

One year after Michael graduated, we sold our house in DeSoto and permanently moved to Horseshoe Bay. It was difficult leaving friends who had been so good to Karen during her illness. Karen was now eager to retire, and I could not wait to play those fabulous golf courses often. Making new friends was never difficult for Karen during any of our previous relocations. The same was true in Horseshoe Bay.

We immediately found a church home at First Baptist Church of Marble Falls. We planned to take a short break from church leadership. However, one Sunday the pastor said that too many people were looking into the mirror asking what the church could do for them. He added that instead we should be looking out the window to see what we could do for others.

Darn. The only thing I could see out that window was that our plan to sit back for a while was disappearing into the horizon.

Fortunately, we were at the right place at the right time. The leader of the young couple's class had moved away from Marble Falls. We were asked if we would be interested in teaching and leading that class. It was a perfect fit for us. There were just a few couples who were involved at the time, and we thought that it was a great opportunity to help develop the future leaders of the church.

Soon, there were 30 to 50 couples attending the class every week. We named the class "The Encouragers." The name appropriately described the members of the class. Those couples, whose ages were between 25 and 45, taught Karen and me a lot. They were experiencing issues with children and work, which created personal stress as they tried to hold their families together. Years later I wrote the book *Second Quarter … Get the Most Out of Life's Toughest Times*, reflecting on challenges those couples experienced and providing inspiration for others to make it through similar tough times.

Karen also began a mom-to-mom ministry in the church. The ministry connected the young moms in our church with women who would mentor them through situations they were facing in their life. Karen was definitely in her element teaching and mentoring young couples. I loved it, too. It was another one of those times when we both believed that we were doing exactly what we should be doing.

Karen was a really good giver but not a very good taker. She would have no part in receiving any sympathy because of her cancer fight. On one occasion, she was asked to speak to a cancer survivor group in Austin about her journey. She proudly told me that her subject was going to be "Things That are Great About Cancer." I told her that would be the shortest speech on earth. She believed that she was purposefully chosen for her cancer journey. She knew exactly what she was going to say to encourage others through their tough times.

And, she did.

Your Grace of Fresh Starts Applied

My mission in life is to encourage others. I have found that for me to be really good at encouraging others, I have to spend most of my energy on people who want to be encouraged.

Believe it or not, many people enjoy being discouragers. Some like to gossip. Some enjoy misery. Some want you to be at least as negative as they are. There is an abundance of discouragers all around us.

Don't go there with them and waste time with those who want to waste your time.

Be mindful of your relationships and the impact they are having on you. You may have to make some tough decisions. You may have to spend less time with a negative, cynical, discouraging person. If allowed, those people will drain you, just like one bad battery will drain the energy from all the other good batteries in a flashlight. Eventually, it becomes difficult to tell which battery was the one that brought all the other good batteries down.

Encouragers will recharge your battery. Love all people, but do not let anyone prevent you from becoming the person you want to be. There is no substitute for surrounding yourself with positive people who care enough to encourage you, suffer with you, and celebrate with you.

fourteen

Grace of Dignity

Karen's Very Best

---

*The greatest legacy one can pass on
to one's children and grandchildren is not money
or other material things accumulated in one's life,
but rather a legacy of character and faith.*
— BILLY GRAHAM

In 2009, things were rolling along.

Jennifer married Kevin Laymance in 2005. A little over a year later, they gave us our first grandchild, Noah David Laymance. Another year or so after that, they had another boy, Pearce, which was Karen's maiden name. Karen and I experienced new and spectacular highlights in our lives when we became grandparents.

Kim married Huntleigh Harris in 2005. Huntleigh survived the shock of meeting his future in-laws for the first time when Karen was chemo bald and I was on the gurney for a quadruple bypass.

Michael was scheduled to graduate on time from Texas A&M in 2009 despite surviving a close call in one course. He did well in school but was even better in extracurricular activities that had nothing to do with academics. The apple did not fall far from the tree in that regard.

CornerStone was rocking and rolling. At church, we were still teaching young adults. I was serving on the long-range planning committee and was the chairman of both the stewardship committee and the pastor search committee at First Baptist Marble Falls. We were very active in our community.

Times were good.

Karen and I continued to go to the oncologist in Austin for monthly checkups. For many months, there was no sign of cancer. Regardless of how hard we tried to prevent cancer from filling our thoughts before each visit, the fear of cancer was always our silent worry.

A few weeks before Michael's graduation, our cancer fear turned into reality. A CAT scan revealed that the cancer was in Karen's lungs and liver. Our oncologist, Dr. Debra Patt, was straightforward. The cancer was incurable and inoperable. We could go through chemo again to stunt the aggression, but it would not eliminate the disease. The average expected lifespan was five years.

That was a mighty blow.

The news would be upsetting to our family, so we decided not to tell anyone for a few weeks until we would see them at Michael's graduation.

The night before Michael's graduation in May 2009, our family was in College Station to celebrate. When we got to our hotel, Kim said that she had a late Mother's Day present for Karen. She and Huntleigh came to our room and gave her a present, which included an Aggie bib and baby shirt. They were expecting their first child.

We were both thrilled with Kim's news. Every time that I glanced over at Karen that evening, she had an ear-to-ear smile on her face. I would wake up in the middle of the night and look at her and she would still be smiling. All night long. Those were among her happiest days.

We had planned a celebration brunch for our family and several of Michael's friends the morning after his graduation. That was the first time that we met Kelley – a beautiful, brunette Aggie – who would eventually become Michael's wife.

We withheld the cancer news from anyone until after Michael's brunch. We broke the news to Kim and Huntleigh in the restaurant parking lot, immediately after brunch. Shortly after our conversation with Kim and Huntleigh, we told Jennifer and Kevin.

We were all devastated.

We chose to wait to tell Michael. He had just graduated, fulfilling one of our hopes and dreams. The day after the brunch, Michael and several of his friends were going to Las Vegas to celebrate their graduation. Breaking the news to him could wait.

I had read some of Pastor Rick Warren's thoughts when his wife was diagnosed with cancer. He said that he used to think that life was hills and valleys. You go through a dark time, then to the mountaintop, back and forth. He said that he doesn't believe that anymore. Rather than life being hills and valleys, he changed his thoughts to life being more like two rails on a railroad track. At all times, you have something good and something bad going on in your life. No matter how bad things are, there is always something good going on at the same time, for which you can be thankful.

That weekend our lives were moving full speed on both rails. On one rail, we were thrilled with Michael's graduation and Kim's pregnancy. While at the same time, on the other rail, we were crushed that Karen's cancer had returned.

Ironically, we later learned that Kim found out she was pregnant on the exact day that we learned that Karen's cancer had returned.

When Michael returned from Vegas, we told him. He was a wreck. He had been home with Karen while she suffered through treatments the first time. He knew how she fought. He suffered with her. He did not want to see that again.

No one knew, but we had already begun chemotherapy the week of Michael's graduation. Karen kept a good attitude, but it was a rough time for us.

Needing Help

I was having a tough time adjusting to our new reality. I was an emotional mess. I visited my doctor and explained my situation. The doctor said that I was under constant stress and that I needed to take care of myself. He suggested that I begin taking prescribed antidepressants to help me through this period of my life.

I resisted his advice to go on antidepressants. I told the doctor, "I am a motivational and inspirational speaker. I can't be on antidepressants." He politely told me that regardless of my profession, I needed help. He assured me that as soon as he thought the medicines were not necessary, he would take me off the antidepressants immediately.

I followed his advice. I later discovered that I was not the only person in my profession who was on antidepressants … not by a long shot. After about six months, my doctor and I concurred that I could begin decreasing, and I eventually eliminated my antidepressants.

TeamKaren

Shortly after Michael's graduation, we visited Kim in Houston to participate in a 5K walk to support one of Huntleigh's lifelong friends, Rick Summers. Rick had suffered from appendiceal cancer. Karen and I were members of TeamRick in the 5K walk. During our drive back to Horseshoe Bay, I mentioned to Karen that we should do something similar to raise awareness of Inflammatory Breast Cancer.

That was the birth of TeamKaren.

One of the girls in our Bible study class, Donna Wilcox, had vast experience in coordinating fund-raisers. She loved Karen and was an organizational machine. She was also on the school board of the First Baptist Christian School. I approached her with the idea of having all of the kids in the school involved in a TeamKaren event. She took the idea and ran with it. I told Donna that for every dollar raised for TeamKaren – which would be given to MD Anderson Cancer Center in Houston – Karen and I would match for First Baptist Christian School.

Suddenly, we had the entire school's students and their parents on board with TeamKaren.

TeamKaren became a huge family event for Marble Falls, Texas. More than 300 people participated in the 5K walk/run. We had fishing tournaments for the kids and silent auctions. Special guests attended our events, including Sara Roberts, our Austin oncologist nurse practitioner, and the head of IBC research for MD Anderson.

During the three years of TeamKaren, we raised more than $100,000 for IBC research at MD Anderson. Karen and I matched that amount for First Baptist Christian School. It was a fun, exciting event that became one of our annual highlights.

Happy Birthday

The chemotherapy path was not smooth. Karen's immune system was weak and her resistance was down. She could not recover as quickly as she had before. Sadly, tests then revealed that the cancer had moved to her brain. The chemo plan was halted for the brain radiation to begin.

We knew that the road was getting shorter.

For her birthday on April 10, 2012, my gift to her was a trip for Karen and three of her best friends. Stephanie Kruger, Cathy Pryor, and Carol Reese all boarded a plane in Austin with Karen to go to Napa and San Francisco. Karen had a fantastic time. She loved being with her friends.

Stephanie, Cathy, Karen, and Carol

When she returned, she was so excited about the trip that she wanted to take me to the same places where she and her friends had just visited. Two weeks later, we were retracing the trip that the girls had taken.

She had always loved traveling, and I think she probably knew this might be her last trip. It was. She enjoyed every minute.

Her Very Best

Karen participated in the joy of the birth of five grandchildren. She also suffered the pain of losing a grandbaby at birth when baby Marlea never breathed a breath outside Jennifer's womb in 2008.

One of the highlights of Karen's life was when Kim and Huntleigh asked her to cut the cord at the birth of both Hunt and Charlotte, their first two children. At Charlotte's birth, a nurse helped Karen, as she did not have the strength to cut the cord herself. It didn't matter; she was thrilled that Kim allowed her to participate in those special moments.

Karen and Charlotte

Michael and Kelley Baxley became engaged. They planned an Austin wedding for September 15, 2012. The events surrounding the engagement and upcoming wedding infused energy into Karen. She and Michael were extremely close, and she was determined to be at her very best for Michael's wedding.

The oncology team worked with us to help Karen be strong at the wedding. By that time, cancer had spread through her body. Her lungs were deteriorating fast. She was on oxygen 24 hours a day. Her lungs needed to be drained about every two weeks.

On the Monday before Michael and Kelley's Saturday wedding, Karen was admitted to the hospital. She was hooked up to fluids to help build as much strength as possible for the wedding. Her lungs were drained to help her breathe easier.

All of our doctors and our family were focused on helping her have the strength to participate in the Friday rehearsal and Saturday wedding.

We checked Karen out of the hospital and into a hotel in Austin on Friday, the day of the rehearsal dinner. She immediately went to bed to rest up for the rehearsal. When she awoke, she was fired up. She got ready and looked terrific. We made it to the church and then to Abel's on the Lake for the rehearsal dinner. The evening went by without a glitch. She did great.

The Saturday wedding was at 4 p.m. Karen stayed in bed until almost 2. I woke her up and helped her get ready. She looked beautiful. We made it to the church in plenty of time.

In the wedding procession, Michael and I escorted Karen to her place on the second row as the mother of the groom. She walked with us down the aisle without her oxygen, beaming the whole way, never coughing even once. That was a remarkable feat. One of the most amazing pictures of her life captured her joy as she walked between Michael and me. She was thrilled. She had accomplished her goal.

Karen's amazing walk at
Michael's wedding

I was honored to be Michael's best man. I helped get Karen seated and hooked back up on oxygen, then I returned to the back of the church for the rest of the procession.

The wedding was perfect. The entire evening, Karen did not cough even one time. Before this night, she had been coughing incessantly. Her radiant smile never left her face. After pictures, we drove to the Austin Club for the reception. Our family's table was up front. We placed Karen in her place for the remainder of the evening.

When it was time for the mother/son dance, we knew that she would not be able to continue for the entire dance. We had spread the word that the dance would be for every mother/ son in attendance. The plan was that when Karen and Michael stopped dancing, all the other moms/sons would take over the dance floor.

The music began with Karen and Michael standing together. There was not much dancing; it was more like hugging. Karen made it through the entire song; there was no need for anyone to finish the dance for her.

Michael's wedding was one of the highlights of her life. Most of her closest friends were there. Everyone had an opportunity to visit with her for a few minutes. She had the same line for everyone, "I'll see you on the other side." She knew that would be the last time she would see most of those friends.

The reception lasted until 10 p.m. that evening. She did not miss a thing. When Michael and Kelley left the reception as a married couple, she was throwing petals, sending the newlyweds off to their new life together.

Karen was at her very best that night.

Thanksgiving

After Michael's wedding, Karen's health took a downward spiral. She was exhausted. She told me that she thought she would make it until Thanksgiving but was not sure how long after that. She was in hospice care and there would be no more cancer treatments.

Her hospital bed in our bedroom was at the foot of our bed. Every night I would take her to bed and lay with my head toward hers and talk with her until we fell asleep. Some nights it was a minute and some nights we would talk for an hour. Cathy Pryor had spent days putting together Karen's favorite songs for her to listen to her on her iPod. She loved listening to that music while we talked each evening. She would recap the memories that we shared in our life together until she fell asleep.

Occasionally, she would burst out in laughter while she was sleeping. It would scare me to death, but that was okay. Our laughing together did not stop until she took her last breath.

A few weeks before Thanksgiving, Kim and her two kids moved in with us for Karen's last days. Things were not going well.

Our family gathered on Thanksgiving with the family pitching in to make a traditional Thanksgiving meal. Even during our painful moments that day, we still had a lot to be thankful for. Karen asked everyone to gather around her. She began telling stories – I am not sure where some of those stories came from – but we all laughed until we cried. At one point, she even burst out into a British accent when telling about one of our England vacations. She also invented several new words during our last conversations that will forever be part of our family vocabulary, such as "floatate," which apparently means sharing cheap things around our house. She specifically wanted Christmas salt-and-pepper shakers to floatate.

She also reminded us that we are family – the good, the bad, and the ugly – although she did not identify who fell into which category. She hilariously delivered her rendition of Sister Sledge's 1979 song "We Are Family."

It was quite a night.

Karen's last meal was our family Thanksgiving meal. She struggled to eat while using a fork in each hand. She fell asleep with a fork in her hand, stuck in her piece of chocolate pie. I woke her and walked with her to bed.

Those were the last steps she took.

All of our family but Kim, her two small children, Evelyn, and Karen's sister, Sandy, left the next day. Everyone was hoping that she would make it to Christmas. It was not to be.

Karen's Legacy

Karen died peacefully in the early morning of December 4, 2012. Her family, our pastor Ross Chandler, Evelyn, Sandy, and Cathy and Al Pryor were by her side.

Karen dug her faith well deep. She truly believed – without a shadow of a doubt – that all things worked together for the good for those who love God. She believed in God's plan for her life and learned to live an abundant life with cancer instead of dying a bitter life from cancer. She believed that when God called her home, it was His timing and that cancer did not take a day from her life – God had the timing in control. She knew that God would not be surprised when she showed up, and she knew that He would welcome her home with open arms.

Karen loved angels – they were displayed throughout our home. More importantly, though, she saw Jesus through many angels here on earth.

She saw Jesus in our neighbors and friends who would bring food.

She saw Jesus in the people who would take her to chemo.

She saw Jesus when friends would get on their knees to visit with her.

She saw Jesus when her friends would travel long distances to spend a few minutes with her in her last days.

She saw Jesus when the church choir came to our house to sing for her.

She saw Jesus when a nurse would comfort her.

She saw Jesus when people were praying for her.

She said that she could hear prayers for her even though the prayers were being offered up for her by friends who were miles away.

She saw Jesus in the angels in her life. However, I truly believe that the reason she saw Jesus in others was because, like looking in a mirror, others could see Jesus in her.

Karen lived with faith, peace, and dignity in everything she did. She was the sweetest person many people will ever know.

She died the same way. There was no bitterness or fear. She was secure in her faith and never wavered.

It was a great privilege to spend 36 years with her.

The Bible says that the fruit of the Spirit is love, joy, peace, forbearance, kindness, goodness, faithfulness, gentleness, and self-control. I believe that every person who knew her, in sickness and in health, would attest that her life was a bountiful harvest of that fruit.

There is an old Indian saying, "When you were born, you cried and the world rejoiced. Live your life in such a manner that when you die, the world cries and you rejoice." That is what she did.

Karen's funeral was on December 6, 2012, in the church she loved so much: First Baptist Marble Falls. More than 500 people attended. People came from every city we had lived in. Five of our previous pastors attended. It was a great tribute to her.

During the service, three students from First Baptist Christian School spoke about the influence Karen had on them and their school. My friend Joe Miles was asked to sing, but he could not come because he was fighting a cancer battle also. Dorey Stubblefield filled in for Joe and did a wonderful job singing "How Great Thou Art" and "I Can Only Imagine." I delivered the eulogy that I had written and shared with Karen during her last days of consciousness. Our friend and pastor, Ross Chandler, spoke an inspirational message of hope. A member of our Bible study class, Sarah Spillman, sang "Blessings."

Karen and I had discussed whom she would choose as pallbearers. I thought that some of my friends – Tod, Ken, Louis, Rocky, Al, Joe, and Ty – would be her choices. She had a different thought. She wanted the "studs" from our Bible study class to be her pallbearers. She loved and respected those men enough that she wanted them to be the last to carry her. At her request, about 30 young men had a part in carrying her body on its last trip.

The service was an inspirational celebration of her life and reflected the eternal hope we have in Jesus.

When Karen was laid to rest, I lost more than a wife. I lost my best friend. Of course, I knew that her time was rapidly approaching, but that did not take away the sting, hurt, or emptiness when reality set in. Losing a loved one is the most difficult experience that anyone will ever face. The greater our love, the more difficult the parting. That is why losing Karen was so hard. My most special gifts are the memories of our life together. They will remain forever. Never does a day pass without me reflecting upon those memories and thanking God for the grace of our time together.

A few days after her funeral, I boarded a plane alone and flew to Las Vegas. That was a comfortable place for me to escape. I knew the city well. No one would know me. I could walk and think at all hours of the night. I slept about 15 hours a day while decompressing from the strain under which I had been living.

It was a scary and lonely time.

After three days, I flew back home. When I walked into my house in Horseshoe Bay, I knew that the home we both loved so much would never be the same.

Your Grace of Dignity Applied

Someone once said that you are either going into a storm, leaving a storm, or you are between storms. I was with Karen in all three of those situations and I can say without hesitation that regardless of which we were in, she faced her situation with grace and dignity.

You will have your own takeaways from this chapter, but here are a few things that I learned while walking with her through her struggle.

First, she always kept her sense of humor. The situation she was facing was not humorous. There was nothing funny at all. Yet, she always managed to find something to lighten the mood for the people around her.

What if you could develop that talent? People would flock to be around you just like they flocked to be around Karen, even in her most painful moments.

Second, she rarely complained. Isn't that amazing? A person who was dying did not spend her time focused on the unfairness of her situation.

What if you made it a point to quit complaining right now? There is a time for constructive criticism, but if it is not constructive, why not just quit complaining right now?

Third, she was optimistic. It sounds sort of crazy that she maintained her positive demeanor even in the most negative situation.

If you had the opportunity to ask her how she maintained her sense of humor, why she seldom complained, and why she was optimistic, I am pretty sure that she would respond: *Why not? Would I feel better or worse if I didn't laugh, complained all the time, or was negative?*

What do you think?

fifteen

Grace of Loving Again

Picking up the Pieces

---

*When I realized that I wanted to spend
the rest of my life with Madeline,
I wanted the rest of my life to start as soon as possible.*

How do you pick up the pieces when you have just lost your lifelong partner? Karen was my glue, and now there were pieces of me scattered all over the place. There are no books or advisers that can tell you what to do, how to act, or where to go.

She and I talked every night for more than 36 years. We both knew what the other was thinking before a word was spoken. That is the way it is in a loving marriage. Our marriage had survived challenges that neither of us could have seen coming when we exchanged vows. Regardless of what came our way, both of us were 100 percent committed to each other.

But, I found myself as a widower. Who knows how to be a "good" widower?

I reached out to a few people for advice.

I called my attorney, Grady Dickens, who had lost his wife, Tonya, about 10 years earlier. I was with him when he received the news that Tonya's cancer was inoperable and incurable. I saw the effect it had on him and his two daughters. Within a year of losing Tonya, Grady married Rhonda, and they seemed to be happy. Grady's quick marriage was a shock to our family and was the subject of several passionate family discussions. I thought his quick marriage was good for him. He would not jump into a relationship without the appropriate due diligence; that was his training as an attorney. I trusted him to make the right choice. Karen and Kim vehemently disagreed and thought that he moved too quickly. Grady told me that only I would know what to do and when.

A pastor friend and confidant of mine, Gene Glazer, told me to not do anything for at least six months. He said that I needed to work my way through the fog and it takes time. Of course, I didn't like his counsel. Six months for a 59-year-old seemed like a long time.

I also leaned on Kim for advice. She and her mom were extremely close, and they had several intimate conversations about what would happen to me. Karen had told Kim that I would need to remarry because I could not make it by myself. Kim naturally resisted that thought, but she knew that I would be a total wreck alone.

Kim came to visit me on January 5, 2013, in Horseshoe Bay. We began talking about my future. She started talking about the types of women who would not fit well with her or the rest of my family. She was talking in jest, or was she? After a while, I said to Kim, "Why don't you tell me exactly what type of person you think fits with us." She quickly came up with 10 characteristics for me to pay attention to when the time came for me to begin dating. I wrote them down.

Kim's list:

1. Widow – I pushed back. There are many more divorced women at my age than widowers. She did not give in. "Dad, only a widow would understand what our family has been through. This is important."

2. Five in front – Her age had to begin with a five as the first number. Now, she had narrowed it down to a widow between 50 and 59. Again, I pushed back, but to no avail.

3. Loves kids – I was all in on that one.

4. Not trying to replace mom – no problem with that, either.

5. Active – Someone who likes to travel and enjoys football – no problem.

6. Optimistic about life – for sure.

7. Location – must live close to Kim. I thought that would probably be a natural since I only lived an hour away from her.

8. No major drama in family – no problem.

9. Youngest kid at least 20 – That tied back to someone who is 50+. Unfair, I thought.

10. Close relationship with her kids – absolutely.

At least I knew what Kim thought.

On January 15, I called an acquaintance, Madeline LeBlanc – the same person whom I worked with at FedEx. Madeline had lost her husband a few years before. She left FedEx several years before me, and I had not seen her in about 25 years.

However, I had spoken to her briefly when her husband, John, had passed. I had met John on a couple of President's Club trips. He was impressive … handsome, athletic, and a successful institutional broker. He died from Lewy Body Dementia at age 56. I read about his passing on an ex-FedEx message board. The board was only active for a short time, but during that time Jean Ward-Jones, a mutual friend of Madeline and mine, had posted that John had passed.

Madeline and John lived in Mandeville, Louisiana. The city is on the north shore of Lake Pontchartrain just outside of New Orleans. I googled her telephone number and gave her a call. Surprisingly, she answered her home phone. I shared the news of Karen's passing. She had heard from some former FedEx people that Karen was sick, but she did not know that Karen had passed.

We talked for a few minutes. Other than the brief conversation that we had when John passed, I had not talked to her in over two decades. Neither of us knew anything about how the other had managed being a caregiver for our spouse.

I told her that I felt lost, empty, and lonely. Knowing that she had been in the place that I just entered, I asked her if she had any advice on how to make it through this new time in my life.

She said that she "got" what I was expressing and how I was feeling. She said that she had been there and was still there. Her simple advice was to take it one day at a time. She said that she was deeply involved with her church and had received solid emotional support from her circle of friends. But, even after more than two years, she said that she still felt the same emotions I expressed. She told me that those emotions would not disappear anytime soon.

Everything I shared with her about my feelings, she would say, "I get it," and proceed to share how she felt as well.

She told me about her three children, Ashley, Melissa, and Michael, and how amazing they had been during John's illness. I shared with her the same sentiments about my family during Karen's illness. Tragedy tends to draw families closer or separate them even further. We both were thankful that our families were drawn closer together during the most stressful time of our lives.

Ironically, she had two older daughters and a son named Michael, just like the kids in my family. That would be the first of many common oddities that we discovered we shared.

I asked her if it would be okay if I called her again. She said sure.

I called the next night. We talked for quite a while. We caught up on any news that we had with our mutual friends from our FedEx days. I asked if she had dated anyone. It had been a while since John's passing, and I thought that she would have a line of guys interested in taking her out. But, she said that the time had not been right for her yet. She said that Melissa recently married and all of her time, energy, and money had gone into that wedding.

She went on to say that her daughters had suggested that she join a Christian singles site. She was not ready for that scene.

I asked if she would mind if I called her again. She said okay. I said that I would call her at 9 p.m. the next evening.

The following evening, I called her at straight-up 9 p.m. She answered immediately. Our deeper conversations revealed that both of our caregiving situations had been remarkably similar. We both "got it."

I stalked Madeline on Facebook. She looked good. She was 56 years old and appeared to be in great physical condition. I thought the pictures may have been from 10 years earlier until I saw pictures from her daughter's wedding. Then, I knew the pictures were recent. She looked happy and proud at the wedding. I could relate to that scene as my son Michael's wedding was exactly two months before Melissa's.

We decided to talk at 9 p.m. the next evening. Our conversations began to flow more easily. Then, we made a decision that I would call her every evening at 9 p.m. until one of us decided to quit talking with the other.

I was eagerly anticipating our call every evening. I think she was, too. What began as a five-minute conversation evolved into several hours every night. It wasn't long before our talks evolved from a focus on the past and our great memories to conversations about our own hopes for the future.

After a few weeks of talking on the phone, I asked her if I could come see her. She said that I should wait a few more weeks and make sure that I was ready to see someone. That evening, she shared that her husband, John, had family in Blanco, Texas, and that for several years their family spent Labor Day there. Blanco was only 30 minutes from Horseshoe Bay. She mentioned that one of John's cousins was Elise Walker. I looked Elise up on Facebook. Ironically, the first friend who appeared on Elise's page was Cathy Pryor, one of Karen's best friends. I was scheduled to have dinner the following night, January 31, 2013, at Ginger & Spice, a local Thai restaurant, with Cathy and her husband, Al, who was one of my best friends. Karen and I had eaten with them at that restaurant many times.

The next evening after dinner, I asked Cathy how she knew Elise. She said that Elise was her daughter Bonnie's sister-in-law. She asked how I knew Elise. I told her that I didn't know Elise, but I had been talking to Madeline. Then, I told the first person, Cathy Pryor, that I was thinking about going to New Orleans to see her sometime soon.

Cathy was one of Karen's closest friends. One thing I love about Cathy is that you always know where you stand with her. She had been by Karen's side during her entire second cancer journey and was still mourning her loss. She was astounded that I had been talking to anyone this soon after Karen's passing. I could tell that she was not happy with me.

Al's reaction was just the opposite. He was happy that I was thinking about going to see someone. He was encouraging. Cathy was speechless, which was rare for her. She loved Karen and was protective of her and our family.

I learned that evening that my friends were going to have some kind of emotional reaction regardless of what I did. And, my guy friends would probably have a completely different reaction than Karen's girlfriends. Cathy and Al provided some insight on how others would feel about any move that I would make.

Madeline and I continued to talk each evening at 9 p.m. Sometimes we would talk for an hour, but most of the time we talked for two, three or four hours. There were a lot of gaps to fill in our lives. We talked openly about John and Karen and how great a partner each had been. We talked a lot about our children and how proud we were of all of them.

We shared recent pictures of our lives. I remember playing golf at Summit Rock in Horseshoe Bay with my regular golf group. (The views on that course are spectacular.) I was taking pictures to share with Madeline a peek of where I lived. One of my golf partners asked if I was a tourist or a golfer. I was not ready to let them know that I was trying to let someone 500 miles away get a glimpse into my life.

Dad Is Going on a Date

After a month of talking, we agreed that it was time to meet face-to-face. We decided that I would come to see her in New Orleans on March 5.

I was still traveling and speaking for my business quite a bit. I promised my kids that I would always let them know my travel schedule. This trip was different. I thought it was important to tell each of them face-to-face, if possible, that I was headed to New Orleans and why I was going.

Jennifer lived about four hours away, so I had to tell her over the phone. She told me that she supported me and gave me her blessing to go.

I went to Austin, about an hour away, to tell Michael and his new bride, Kelley. When I told them, Michael froze. He literally froze. It was like he passed out with his eyes open. Kelley was supportive and tried to thaw him out. Michael was not angry; he was just stunned. His message to me was to be careful.

The night Michael froze.

I chose to tell Kim on Valentine's Day when I would be at her house for dinner. I was real nervous because I wasn't sure how she would react. Earlier that evening, I had noticed that Kim was eating Twizzlers. I thought that was odd. She normally did not sit around and eat candy, even on Valentine's Day. Eating Twizzlers was even more strange.

Kim had some big news of her own. Her two children were wearing shirts that read: Big Brother Hunt and Big Sister Charlotte. It took me a while to catch on to Kim's magnificent news that she was expecting another baby.

I waited until her two kids were in bed and I finally gathered the nerve to tell her about my upcoming trip. She took the news better than I had imagined. Her pregnancy was fantastic news and it softened the shocking news that I shared.

Ironically, Kim told me that she was pregnant with Hunt the day before we shared that Karen's cancer returned. Now, about five years later, she was telling me about her third child's pregnancy on the same day that I told her that I was going to see another woman. It was a strange coincidence.

By the end of Valentine's Day, all my family knew that I was going to visit Madeline on March 5.

About the same time, Madeline told her kids. It had been two-and-a-half years since John's passing and her kids were excited that their mom was going out on a date. They wanted to know all the details about me, and they helped her plan the activities for my visit. They were happy to see Madeline's spirit light up again.

Face-to-face

On March 5, I boarded a plane from Austin to New Orleans. I was excited but felt guilty at the same time. I had to convince myself that I was not being disloyal to Karen. She would be okay with this trip under the circumstances. It was still a very, very strange feeling.

Madeline met me at the airport. Thank goodness her Facebook pictures were recent and accurate. She looked terrific. Our first meeting was mega-awkward. Although we had talked for hours on the phone, our face-to-face words did not flow as freely. The situation made us feel a little weird and uncomfortable. It was a tough adjustment mentally and emotionally for both of us.

Madeline had made reservations at R'evolution, a new restaurant in the French Quarter. This restaurant was located inside the Royal Sonesta Hotel. It was just down the street from where Karen and I spent our honeymoon 37 years before.

We arrived in the French Quarter about an hour before our dinner reservation. Madeline was driving, and she parked the car about a block from the restaurant. Then, we went for a walk along the banks of the Mississippi. It was a clear, warm evening. It was not nearly as humid as I remembered from my numerous business trips to the city.

During our walk, we passed one of the famous Lucky Dogs hotdog stands. I remember thinking that even though I would never eat one of those hot dogs, I was a lucky dog to be there.

Shortly after those thoughts, I found out that I was not the luckiest dog in town. There was a "magician" working close to where we were walking who won five bucks from me. He bet me that he knew where I got my shoes. I said, "You're on."

He looked at me and smiled. "You got 'em on your feet right here in New Orleans."

We laughed. I felt pretty stupid. I gave him the money.

We meandered farther on down the walkway and sat on a park bench. It was a picture-perfect evening and we enjoyed a nice breeze drifting off the river. We listened to jazz music coming from the decks of the riverboats as we watched their paddlewheels propel the massive boats by. When they blew their steam whistles, it sounded as though the boats were right next to where we were sitting.

Our conversation on the park bench took place in-between several awkward pauses. But, it was good. I gave Madeline a small gift. It was a silver bracelet that had three words: *faith, hope,* and *love.* I was not sure where our relationship was headed, but I knew that regardless of where we went, we could both use a healthy dose and reminder of those three traits.

Shortly after I gave her the bracelet, it was time for dinner, and we walked to R'evolution. While we were at dinner, our conversation began to flow more naturally. It had been a long time since either of us had been at a nice restaurant, with or without our spouse. It was weird, but it felt good at the same time.

Upon leaving the restaurant, Madeline drove the 24 miles across Lake Pontchartrain to her home in Mandeville.

Before leaving Texas, I jokingly told Kim that if the date did not go well, I would be jumping out of the car into Lake Pontchartrain. While on the Lake Pontchartrain bridge, I received this text from Kim: "On a scale of 1-10, how are things going?" My text back: "10+".

I was not going to jump.

For the record, Madeline scored eight out of the 10 on Kim's list. She missed on living close to Kim, and I discovered later that Madeline's enjoyment of football is a little questionable.

I stayed at the Marriott Courtyard, which was only about 10 minutes from Madeline's home.

Madeline had our next day planned. She had invited her kids to meet us at Dakota Restaurant in Mandeville. I had seen the girls when they were toddlers and Michael once as a baby. I was pretty nervous.

Melissa had flown in earlier in the week from her home in Virginia Beach. In the first of many role reversals, Melissa and Ashley went shopping with their mom to help select her wardrobe for this special weekend. Their selection of clothing was really good.

First time to meet
Madeline's kids

Madeline and I pulled into Dakota's parking lot at the exact same time as Michael. He parked his big pickup truck next to Madeline's car. As he got out of his truck, I was taken back by his resemblance to his father. This tall and handsome young man looked exactly as I had remembered John. We enjoyed the time with Michael before the girls arrived. He was a nice, polite, pleasant, and impressive young man.

Ashley and Melissa arrived fashionably late. They both were beautiful. Ashley had Madeline's easy smile, and Melissa's appearance reminded me of Madeline when I first met her years ago. During our short time together that night, it was evident that Madeline's children were well-balanced, kind, and wonderful adults. Madeline and John raised them well.

I was happy to meet Madeline's children, and I think the feeling was mutual. They had no idea that things were going to blast off as fast as they were. We didn't either.

A couple of weeks later, Madeline boarded a plane for Texas. We had dinner with Michael and Kelley. Michael had thawed out by then and it was a nice evening. We went to see Jennifer and her family in East Texas, where Madeline also met my two sisters, who were living in the area. Jennifer was happy that her dad was dating.

First date in Texas

Kim and Huntleigh invited us to their home for dinner. Kim had two little ones running around the house and was pregnant with her third. It was a pleasant meeting. Madeline and Kim spoke a lot about Karen. As with Madeline's girls the week before, Kim was in the parental mode of trying to figure out what was going on with her dad. Thank goodness, Madeline and Kim got along well.

Although Madeline and I never discussed it, we both understood that if any of our kids detected major issues, our dating would come to a screeching halt. Instead of a halt, the relationship accelerated.

On my next trip to Louisiana, I met Madeline's extended family. I already knew her sister, Jaime. She had worked with me at FedEx. We enjoyed getting reacquainted and shared some old stories. Jaime could vouch for me with Madeline's mom, sister Karen, and brother Keith. I also met seven of Madeline's closest girlfriends at a restaurant, which was interesting to say the least.

Madeline's next trip to Texas included meeting Stephanie Kruger, Joe Miles, my pastor and friend, Ross Chandler, and my CornerStone team. If we got serious, we wanted to know how all the pieces fit together.

Engaged at the Post Office

We were serious. A couple of weeks before while we were in Louisiana, I had spotted a ring that I thought was perfect for Madeline if we were to get engaged. I told the jeweler to take a picture of it, and if I called him, he could send it to me. On April 15, I made the call to the jeweler. I asked him to send it to my Post Office box in Horseshoe Bay to arrive on April 17.

On the morning of April 17, Madeline and I had an appointment with an attorney in Marble Falls to understand our legal options if we were to marry. On the way toward his office, he called and stated that he had a family emergency and postponed the appointment. I turned the car around and drove to the Horseshoe Bay post office. In my P.O. Box was a notice that I had a package that required my signature. I took the notice to the front desk and retrieved the package from the postal worker at the counter. The engagement ring was in the box.

Returning to my car, I immediately asked Madeline to marry me. The middle of the Post Office parking lot might not have been the most romantic place for an engagement, but it was the quickest place.

We conferenced Madeline's kids in on the phone and told them the news. We told my family quickly, as well. We were excited.

We could see hope and a future.

We first laid eyes on each other on March 5. We were engaged April 17. Some people thought that was a little fast. Imagine that. We knew it was fast, too, but I don't think we realized how fast it really was until we looked back. At the time, we were in a full-time courting mode. When we were not together, we were on the phone talking. We covered a lot of ground in a few short weeks, and we had a little head start by knowing each other many years before.

I think even more importantly, though, was that both of us had really good marriages for over 30 years apiece. We knew how to be married well, had done it, and we frequently talked about why our marriages worked so well. In addition, at this stage of our lives, we each had more than 50 years of observing many other marriages and relationships. We could not talk about or predict everything that was in our future, but we had a wealth of experience to guide our own due diligence about each other.

Our family and friends were pleased that we were dating, until we got serious. Then our closest friends and family raised legitimate questions and concerns: Did we know what we were doing? Had we considered the distance between our families? What about holidays? Are we sure? Why so fast? And, many other questions. They were scared and protective of us and did not want us to make a mistake. I do not think anyone had an issue with the new person who would be coming into their life, but they probably had issues with the new situation that may be happening to their lives. And, I believe a common fear among all six of our children was that we would forget about our last spouse because we had a new one. Nothing could be further from the truth, but it was a legitimate fear that I think they all shared.

Our children loved both of their parents. It was healthy that they were concerned.

Kim's due date was the first week of October. The latest that she would be able to travel would be the first week of August. We set our wedding day for August 3 so that Kim could be at our wedding.

Between April 17 and August 3, Madeline and I tried to meet as many people and fill in as many gaps in our lives as we could. We wanted our friends to meet us face-to-face and have some assurance that we were going to be okay.

Baby Elle

Our most challenging time during the engagement involved Kim's pregnancy. Five months into her pregnancy, the doctors informed Kim that the baby was not going to survive the pregnancy. Kim's amniotic fluid was low; the baby was not moving and had stopped growing. There was no hope. They instructed Kim to go home and let nature take its course. The baby's heart was not expected to continue to beat more than a week or so.

Our plans for the wedding were still on for August 3, but we prepared to postpone.

Fortunately, Kim did not go home and wait for nature to

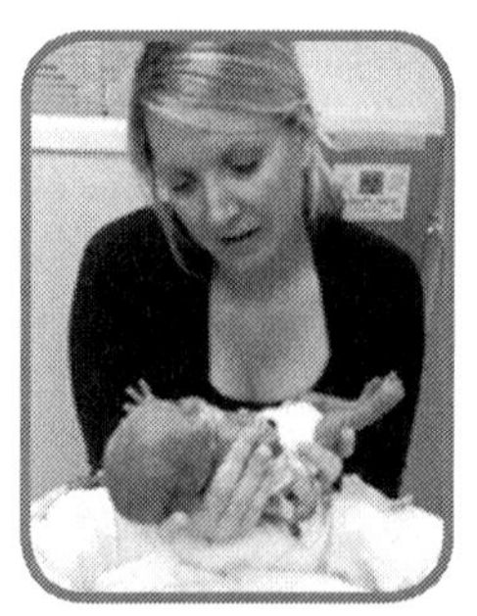

take its course. She put herself on bed rest, drank gallons of water every day, summoned prayer warriors, and left the baby's future in God's hand.

On July 26, exactly one week before our wedding, baby Elle was born, weighing in at two pounds, three ounces. Elle was to spend several months in the NICU before she came home perfectly healthy to Kim, Huntleigh, Hunt, and Charlotte in October.

On August 3, 2013, Madeline and I were married. It was a good day.

Building Together

Merging our two families was not without challenges. I think that any family who loses a person they loved dearly would have a difficult time adjusting to a new and different family dynamic.

Madeline and I planned to split our time between Louisiana and Texas. We both loved our existing homes, which contained beautiful memories of life with our deceased spouses.

Madeline's children had grown up in her house. Many of their childhood memories were stored in the nooks and crannies of their home. No one could blame them if they preferred for us to continue to live where their memories remained.

My kids were not as attached to Horseshoe Bay. They did not grow up in that house. Several years before, we had moved away from the home that contained most of their childhood memories. Regardless, they had special memories in Horseshoe Bay, as well.

The reality for Madeline and me was that it would be difficult for either of us to ever claim one of those homes as our home. It would always be Karen's kitchen and closets or John's bedroom and workout area. We decided that the best thing to do was to start fresh together in new homes in both cities.

Our families respected our decision and none of our children expressed an objection as we began preparations to build new homes.

In Texas, we found the perfect lot to build our new home in Cordillera Ranch, outside of Boerne, Texas. The lot was on a golf course and was within walking distance of the clubhouse. It was in a double-gated, lock-and-leave community, which took away the worry of leaving it for extended periods of time. Our new location would be 20 minutes from Kim's and an hour-and-a-half from Michael's. Jennifer eventually moved to San Antonio, making her family less than an hour away.

We found another perfect lot to build on in Covington, Louisiana. This lot was in a gated community of only 50 homes. We looked forward to living there and believed it was another safe place to leave for an extended period of time.

The building of two houses, 500 miles apart, began at the same time. Our thinking was that if our marriage could sustain building two homes at once, we could sustain almost anything.

We were blessed to have two good builders and an incredible designer. Rachelle Woodard is a very close friend of Madeline's and is the most talented decorator I have ever seen. Rachelle was the quarterback for both of our building projects. She knew Madeline's taste and figured out my taste as we went along. Because of Rachelle and our responsive builders at Cordillera and Covington, both of the projects were pleasant experiences.

Our new homes were far greater than we could have ever
visualized.

Newly Wed Families

Madeline and I are both extremely proud of each of our
children. With our marriage, we each inherited another
wonderful family to love and nurture. It is gratifying that
they have stuck by us, even when it was difficult for them
to understand our situation. Our families are a beautiful
reflection of the loving nature of Karen and John.

Our new life together was foreign and different to Madeline
and me, as well. We have both had to learn that doing some
things differently is okay. We have learned to sacrifice for each
other. We have learned that we will not be able to participate
in every grandkid's birthday or every family event. We have
learned that times of mourning for our spouses can pop up
any time. We know that we each think of our former spouses
every day, and that is okay.

Neither of us would want to begin our relationship all over
again, but given the chance again, we happily and gratefully
would jump right in.

Our married life has been a whirlwind. We moved into both
of our new homes in 2015. We brought an abundance of
great memories and traditions from our old homes. We see
and feel Karen and John's positive influence on us and our
children. We believe that they would be happy with how we
have embraced each of their children.

When we married, Madeline immediately became Nana to my
grandchildren, Hunt, Charlotte, Elle, Noah, Pearce, and Asa.
She has taken each of those children as her own.

Cottrell and LeBlanc family (2017)

Our marriage has experienced several major family events. Ashley married David Curtin on December 5, 2014. Kim and Huntleigh had another baby girl, Audrey, on April 2, 2015. Madeline's son, Michael, married Britany Dupaquier on April 16, 2016. Michael and Kelley have had two sons: Garrett David, born on June 17, 2016, and Bradley Scott, who was born on March 27, 2018. In 2017, we also suffered together the loss of Madeline's mom at age 91.

Our family is our greatest grace on earth, and through it all, it did not divide. It multiplied. What greater privilege could we possibly have?

Your Grace of Loving Again Applied

Many people say that widows and widowers who have experienced good marriages tend to remarry much sooner than those whose first marriages were not so great. That makes sense to me. If you had a rough marriage, you probably would not be eager to dive into another marriage, fearing that it might be similar to your previous experience.

If you are a widow, widower, or divorced, I believe that you can love again. I believe that you can live the remainder of your life with hope and a positive future. I believe that you can share laughs with another person again. I believe that you are meant to enjoy living all of your life.

I hope that you can find the right person to love again.

If you are a family member of a widow, widower, or divorcee, I encourage you to give your loved one your blessing to love again. You may feel awkward and uncomfortable for a while. Try to work your way through those feelings.

My time as a widower was short. It did not take long to discover that loneliness is overwhelming. Loneliness consumed my thoughts and never went away. I have read that grief is love that has nowhere to go. For me, it was a painful and sorrowful way to live.

If your loved one finds another person to love, I hope that you will give that person a fair shot to move forward.

One of the greatest gifts that our children and extended family have ever given us was their blessing of our marriage. I am sure it was not easy for them to see mom, dad, brother, or sister married to someone they hardly knew. I can't imagine how I would have felt or reacted if I were in their shoes. However, as Madeline and I reflect on the beginning of our relationship to today, the love and acceptance from both sides of our families has been a magnificent demonstration of an abundance of grace upon grace.

sixteen

Grace of Today

Acknowledging Grace

*My life is a tattered fabric woven together seamlessly
by God's grace upon grace.*

When I began writing this autobiography, I had no idea what
was ahead. I am grateful that I decided that the project was
worth doing, even if it was only for my own musing. Without
writing this book, I am not sure if I would have ever taken the
time to look back and humbly and thankfully consider the
series of events that led me to where I am today.

If you think your life is void of grace, take a look around.
Grace happens to you every day, regardless of what you are
going through.

Several years ago during the Christmas season, a friend gifted
our family with a "Blessings Jar." The jar was a beautiful, clear,
empty jar. The gift box also contained a package of small,
colorful stones. The instructions were simple: Every time we
acknowledged a blessing, thank God for that blessing, and
place a stone in the jar.

This jar took a prominent place in our home as we began to follow those directions. Some of the blessings were huge – like good reports from the doctor. Some were smaller – like how I made three birdies playing golf that day.

Quickly the jar began filling up. Our awareness of blessings had increased, revealing obvious blessings coming from all directions.

We shared our jar when friends came to visit. They would tell a blessing and place a stone in the jar. Eventually we had to purchase more stones and another jar.

The jar was beautiful and thoughtful, but the real gift was the *gift of awareness.* We began to recognize graces around us that we previously overlooked or took for granted.

Maybe your family would like to try a Blessings Jar. The type of jar or stones you use is not important. What *does matter* is the moment you take to acknowledge the grace of today.

Look around. Pay attention. Grace is surrounding you.

Take Others With You

A couple of questions that I am asked most often are:

1. How did you keep going during your most stressful time?

2. How did you get in front of an audience and talk about success, positive attitude, encouragement, and becoming your best while you were living your worst moments?

One answer could be that I just kept putting one foot in front of the other. That is true, but I think there is another answer as well.

Other people were walking with me. I had to depend on other people to build me up and encourage me. Many of those people were from my local church. Being with them and teaching them every week was my soil for maintaining a healthy spiritual life.

It would have been easy for me to stay home and listen to some great sermons on television or online. I would have been comfortable sitting in my favorite chair. I could have justified that listening alone at home, or enjoying solitude on a lake or golf course, or walking a wooded path, was the same as being involved in a worship service, but I knew the truth. You can't worship by proxy. To hear more from God, to know more about God, and to walk closer to God requires that I go where His Word is taught.

Many times in my life, a sermon has positively changed my life. I couldn't have predicted when those special moments would come. I might not have wanted to attend church on those particular days, but had I not gone, I would have missed a life-changing moment. I had to be there to receive the gift of encouragement and a fresh start.

Regardless of how far away you may have wandered, right now is a good time for you to experience your grace of encouragement and fresh start.

Small Stories Inside the Big Story

It is incomprehensible to understand how our small stories fit into God's big story until you look backward. There were many forks in the road where I could have easily taken a different path. When I reflect on how each road led to another road, which led to another road, it is overwhelming.

How could this have happened without God's grace upon God's grace? It couldn't.

From the grace of being born into a wonderful, God-loving family

To the grace of landing the perfect job right out of college

To the grace of being married to an incredible partner for 36 years

To the grace of being in the right place at the right time when Xerox began a new division

To the grace of FedEx beginning a new division that could utilize my gifts and talents

To the grace of FedEx providing jobs for all employees from my division when it failed

To the grace of my experience at the National Spirit Group

To the grace of having the resources to begin CornerStone

To the grace of Mark Layton's role in helping CornerStone continue

To the grace of God's gift of *Monday Morning Leadership* during one weekend in Toronto

To the grace of being a father and grandfather

To the grace of Karen witnessing each of our children's weddings and six of our grandchildren's births

To the grace of Madeline coming into my life

To the grace of John's positive legacy

To the grace of writing this book

To the grace of you reading my story

Don't Blink

Six-and-a-half decades appear to be a real long time, until you have lived it. It seems like a short time ago that I was riding my grandfather's horse, or playing high school football on a Friday night. It seems only days ago that I had brown hair.

Looking backward, the years flew by.

There is a popular song by Kenny Chesney titled "Don't Blink." He sings, "*Just like that you're six years old and you take a nap and you wake up and you're 25 … so don't blink.*" I can relate to that.

I look around and see my kids are the age that I think I should be. My grandchildren are the age that, in my mind, my children should be.

What happened?

Was I blinking all along and missed everyone growing up – including me? I don't think so. I was immersed in my children's activities all of their lives. Looking back, though, it seems I blinked and now they are grown and have their own children.

I encourage you to not blink for a while. Open your eyes … wide open. Don't blink; share with your family how much they mean to you. Don't blink; tell the people at work how thankful you are for your job. Don't blink; admire the beauty of God's creation. Don't blink; give thanks that we are free to live in the greatest country in the world.

Don't blink. Enjoy the grace of today. Take every breath God gives you, and passionately pursue His will for your life. No remorse, no regrets. All in. All the time. If you do, you will discover with astonishment, amazement, and humbleness – as I did – God's amazing grace upon amazing grace.

*Each of you should use whatever gift you have received
to serve others, as faithful stewards
of God's grace in its various forms.*

1 PETER 4:1

Appendix

Photo Album

Quotes From David Cottrell

Inspirational Passages From the Bible

Acknowledgements

Other Books by David Cottrell

About the Author

Photo Album

Grandkids (2018)

Jennifer, Kevin, Noah, Asa, Pearce (2018)

Kim, Huntleigh, Hunt, Charlotte,
Elle, Audrey (2017)

Michael, Kelley, Garrett, Bradley (2018)

Ashley and David (2017)

Melissa (2018)

Michael and Brittany (2017)

Pastor and friend,
Ross Chandler

Golf at Cordillera with
Tod Taylor

Golf Camp Whistling Straits (2016)
Bryan Lancaster, Bill Olsen,
Robert Gillingham

Golf Camp Pebble Beach (2018)
David Murrah, Paul Liberato,
Arlen Espinal, Jay Meral

Former FedEx managers
Tod Taylor, Ken Carnes,
Ty Deleon, Rodger Baca

Evelyn, Sherry, and Mom
at Kim's wedding

Madeline, John, and family (2009)

Madeline and John,
wedding (1978)

Beach Party (2016)

Cottrell Clan (2016)

Grandkids (2017)

2016

2013

2014

2017

Quotes From David Cottrell's Books

Don't be so busy making a living that you forget how to live. Work hard to be successful, but enjoy the journey.
— *Monday Morning Choices*

We all need people who will help us look at situations from a different perspective.
— *Monday Morning Leadership*

The past does not have a future, but you do. Don't let your past eat your future.
— *The Nature of Excellence*

Success is ultimately realized by people who make more right choices … and recover quickly from their bad choices.
— *Monday Morning Choices*

One of the major sources of stress, anxiety, and unhappiness comes from feeling like your life is out of control.
— *175 Ways to Get More Done in Less Time*

When you depend on another's perceptions to match your expectations, you're setting yourself up for disappointment.
— *Monday Morning Leadership*

Doing the right thing isn't always easy, in fact sometimes it's real hard, but just remember that doing the right thing is always right.

— Monday Morning Leadership

Guard your integrity as if it's your most precious possession, because that is what it is.

— Monday Morning Leadership

Integrity is never being ashamed of your reflection.

— The Nature of Excellence

So much of life is about attitude and how we handle what life throws our way. Life is good — even when a situation appears to be the worst.

— Monday Morning Choices

Every grand entrance is preceded by an exit. Focus on the entrance of your future while you are working through the exit of your past.

— Monday Morning Choices

The success of any change depends, in large measure, on your attitude about that change.

— The First Two Rules of Leadership

There is no "grand conspiracy" preventing you from accomplishing what you need to do.

— Monday Morning Choices

You will never have enough time to do everything you need to do, so what you need is a crystal-clear understanding of the important things you have to do.

— Time!

Don't stifle your career by limiting your knowledge.
— *Monday Morning Mentoring*

If you want to be around people who are positive and enthusiastic and eager to live life, your attitude has to be the same.
— *Monday Morning Choices*

Successful people keep moving, even when they are discouraged and have made mistakes.
— *The First Two Rules of Leadership*

There is no problem that is unique to you.
— *Monday Morning Leadership*

Frequently, the difference between success and failure is the resolve to stick to your plan long enough to win.
— *Monday Morning Choices*

Be careful with those you choose to surround yourself. You will become like the people who you spend the most time with.
— *LeaderShift … Making Leadership Everyone's Business*

Passion exposes possibilities.
— *The Nature of Excellence*

Your comfort zone can be your greatest enemy to your potential.
— *Second Quarter … Get the Most Out of Life's Toughest Times*

Give away everything you have learned. If for no other reason, do it selfishly; in order to get more, you must give more.
— *Monday Morning Mentoring*

Go as far as you can see. When you get there, you will know what to do next.
— *LeaderShift … Making Leadership Everyone's Business*

The antidote to fear is knowledge.

    — SECOND QUARTER … GET THE MOST OUT OF LIFE'S TOUGHEST TIMES

If each Monday morning you make the choice to move into the new work week with renewed commitment and passion, you can change all areas of your life. You can truly change your Mondays and change your life.

    — MONDAY MORNING CHOICES

If expecting something in return is your reason for giving, you are really not giving – you're swapping. If you receive something in return for your gift, what you receive is a bonus – not a repayment of a debt.

    — THE FIRST TWO RULES OF LEADERSHIP

In every situation there are always choices – if you choose to see them. If you choose to put on the blinders of victimization, prepare to accept the disappointments that come when you fail to achieve the success you deserve.

    — MONDAY MORNING CHOICES

Bad news never improves with age.

    — LEADERSHIFT … MAKING LEADERSHIP EVERYONE'S BUSINESS

I have never heard anyone say that they wanted to be around more negative, cynical people. Never. Not once.

    — THE FIRST TWO RULES OF LEADERSHIP

One of your most important answers to a question is "I don't know. What do you think?"

    — LEADERSHIFT … MAKING LEADERSHIP EVERYONE'S BUSINESS

Without purpose, you drift. There is no reason to work just to get tired.

    — LEADERSHIFT … MAKING LEADERSHIP EVERYONE'S BUSINESS

The more you learn, the more you earn.
— *Becoming the Obvious Choice*

If you're not happy about how things are, choose to do something about it. For a better tomorrow, do something different today.
— *Monday Morning Choices*

Many times the longest route is taking the short cut.
— *LeaderShift … Making Leadership Everyone's Business*

Without a doubt, success breeds criticism from all corners … and we need criticism to reach our full potential. The trick is to embrace criticism as teaching tools from which we can polish our skills and ideas. Criticism is a gift … learn from it!
— *Monday Morning Choices*

Choosing to search for the truth and having the courage to confront the hard realities will pay dividends to your career. You'll find the road to success a little straighter, the challenges less overwhelming and fewer surprises along the way.
— *Monday Morning Choices*

Many people use the words "integrity" and "honesty" interchangeably. Integrity is a much broader term, coming from the word "integral," which means "whole or undivided." If you have integrity, you are a complete person … without it, you're fragmented and incomplete.
— *The First Two Rules of Leadership*

You must let go to grow.
— *The Nature of Excellence*

Complacency is the root of mediocrity, and mediocrity is success's worst enemy — a far greater enemy, in fact, than failure.
— *Monday Morning Motivation*

Never in history has a situation improved on its own while people sat there doing nothing.
— *Tuesday Morning Coaching*

Knowledge will not come looking for you. You have to seek it out.
— *Becoming the Obvious Choice*

Going the extra mile isn't that much harder than doing what is required. In fact, it is often easier because there are not many people traveling the extra mile … so few, in fact, that you may find yourself alone.
— *Tuesday Morning Coaching*

Most people who are unhappy in life are unhappy because they don't have goals or a sense of purpose.
— *Tuesday Morning Coaching*

Consciously attack procrastination by having the mindset that there is no better time to get things done than right now.
— *Tuesday Morning Coaching*

The most successful people consistently ask themselves, "Is this the best use of my attention at this moment?"
— *Winners Always Quit*

Many people fall into a victim mentality whenever something disrupts concentration … something that seems to be out of their control. They may even think that there's a grand conspiracy preventing them from doing what needs to be done. In reality, they are their own worst enemy. No matter the situation, you control the next move.
— *The First Two Rules of Leadership*

The paradox of change: The best time to do it is when it seems the least necessary.
— *Listen Up, Leader!*

Forgiveness is a gift without attachments.
— *Second Quarter … Get the Most Out of Life's Toughest Times*

The encouraging news is that beyond every exit can be a grand entrance to the abundance God has set before us.
— *Second Quarter … Get the Most Out of Life's Toughest Times*

You can't be the person you want to be without being all in, all the time. No middle ground exists.
— *Second Quarter … Get the Most Out of Life's Toughest Times*

The best way to increase knowledge is to teach someone else.
— *Tuesday Morning Coaching*

You give more so that you will have more to give.
— *Tuesday Morning Coaching*

Most people are not committed enough to make excellence an everyday event.
— *Tuesday Morning Coaching*

People are searching for consistency – where values do not change based on the situation of the day.
— *Tuesday Morning Coaching*

When a person sacrifices his integrity, nothing else really matters.
— *Tuesday Morning Coaching*

It's rare that someone regrets giving it their all, even if it doesn't work out.
— *Tuesday Morning Coaching*

Those who say they are worried sick or worried to death are probably right.
— *Second Quarter … Get the Most Out of Life's Toughest Times*

Never leave a problem … instead, move toward an opportunity.
— *TUESDAY MORNING COACHING*

The true measure of success is being able to look in the mirror and know that you had the courage to live the values that are above all else in your life.
— *TUESDAY MORNING COACHING*

It's okay to fail – everyone fails at some point – but it's not okay to keep failing.
— *TUESDAY MORNING COACHING*

In times of stress and/or ambiguity, never make long-term, life-changing decisions.
— *TUESDAY MORNING COACHING*

Press on. Your defining moment may arrive just when you feel surrounded by adversity.
— *THE NATURE OF EXCELLENCE*

Life may knock you down, but God will never abandon you. No matter what faith test you experience, it has value. Faith tests are a necessary part of your life as you become complete.
— *SECOND QUARTER … GET THE MOST OUT OF LIFE'S TOUGHEST TIMES*

Some things you learn best while in the middle of a storm.
— *TUESDAY MORNING COACHING*

Life is too short not to be happy and too long not to do well.
— *BECOMING THE OBVIOUS CHOICE*

Difficult always comes before easy.
— *TUESDAY MORNING COACHING*

It is never a good idea to lie to yourself, no matter how painful the truth may be.
— Tuesday Morning Coaching

Successful people are not distracted by their success. They are focused on mastering a combination of several simple truths that – put together – create ongoing success.
— Tuesday Morning Coaching

Keeping an open mind to different alternatives will expose opportunities that you did not even know existed.
— Tuesday Morning Coaching

Success is not about luck or the economy ... it is about making a conscious choice that No Matter What happens, you will keep moving forward toward your goals.
— Tuesday Morning Coaching

Change is painful and requires discipline and commitment – but in the long run, improvement cannot be made without change.
— The Next Level

The pain of regret for not being prepared for an opportunity will last far longer than the pleasure of today's laziness.
— Becoming the Obvious Choice

The obvious choice is someone who has the courage to take action.
— Becoming the Obvious Choice

The obvious choice for a promotion is the person who began their preparation long before the new job was even conceived.
— Becoming the Obvious Choice

Ask yourself ... Am I worth following?
— The Magic Question

Establish integrity as your top priority. It should be the cornerstone of all your actions and decisions.

— *MANAGEMENT INSIGHTS*

Stay focused. Discover what is most important ... then stick to it.

— *THE NATURE OF EXCELLENCE*

The average person has great intentions of making a difference. Intentions do not accomplish anything. The people who find success make the conscious decision to step out and make a difference.

— *THE FIRST TWO RULES OF LEADERSHIP*

Change the way you look at things, and things will change the way they look.

— *THE NATURE OF EXCELLENCE*

Favorite Inspirational Passages From the Bible

(NIV translation unless noted)

For I know the plans I have for you, declares the Lord, plans to prosper you and not to harm you, plans to give you hope and a future. JEREMIAH 29:11

No eye has seen, no ear has heard, no mind has conceived what God has prepared for those who love him. 1 CORINTHIANS 2:9

Whatsoever things are true, whatsoever things are honest, whatsoever things are just, whatsoever things are pure, whatsoever things are lovely, whatsoever things are of good report, if there be any virtue, and if there be any praise, think on these things. PHILIPPIANS 4:8 (KJV)

For our light and momentary troubles are achieving for us an eternal glory that far outweighs them all. So we fix our eyes not on what is seen, but on what is unseen, since what is seen is temporary, but what is unseen is eternal. HEBREWS 11:6

Trust in the Lord with all your heart and lean not on your own understanding; in all your ways acknowledge Him, and He will make your paths straight. PROVERBS 3:5-6

I can do everything through Him who gives me strength.
PHILIPPIANS 4:13

No temptation has seized you except what is common to man.
And God is faithful; He will not let you be tempted beyond
what you can bear. But when you are tempted, He will also
provide a way out so that you can stand up under it.
1 CORINTHIANS 10:13

Command those who are rich in His present world not to be
arrogant nor to put their hope in wealth, which is so uncertain,
but to put their hope in God, who richly provides us with
everything for our enjoyment. 1 TIMOTHY 6:17

When you pass through the waters, I will be with you; and
when you pass through the rivers, they will not sweep over
you. When you walk through the fire, you will not be burned,
the flames will not set you ablaze. ISAIAH 43:2

Blessed is the man who perseveres under trial, because when he
has stood the test, he will receive the crown of life that God has
promised to those that love Him. JAMES 1:12

Wait on the Lord: be of good courage, and He shall
strengthen thine heart. PSALMS 27:14

And my God will meet all of your needs according to His glorious
riches in Christ Jesus. Philippians 4:19

You need to persevere so that when you have done the will of
God, you will receive what He has promised. HEBREWS 10:36

Be strong and courageous. Do not be terrified, do not be
discouraged, for the Lord your God will be with you wherever you
go. JOSHUA 1:9

Do you know that in a race all the runners run, but only one gets the prize? Run in such a way as to get the prize.
1 CORINTHIANS 9:24

Let us not become weary in doing good, for at the proper time we will reap a harvest if we do not give up. GALATIANS 6:8-9

But one thing I do! Forgetting what is behind and straining toward what is ahead, I press on toward the goal to win the prize for which God has called me heavenward in Christ Jesus.
PHILIPPIANS 3:13-14

When I am afraid, I will trust in you. PSALM 56:3

But those who hope in the Lord will renew their strength. They will soar on wings like eagles, they will run and not grow weary, they will walk and not faint. ISAIAH 40:31

Do your best to present yourself to God as one approved, a workman who does not need to be ashamed and who correctly handles the word of truth. 2 TIMOTHY 2:15

May the God of hope fill you with all joy and peace as you trust in Him, so that you may overflow with hope by the power of the Holy Spirit. ROMANS 15:13

Peace I leave with you; my peace I give you. I do not give to you as the world gives. Do not let your hearts be troubled and do not be afraid. JOHN 14:27

Whoever wants to be great among you must be your servant. And whoever wants to be greatest of all must be the slave of all. MARK 10:43-44 (LB)

It is more blessed to give than to receive. ACTS 20:35

He heals the brokenhearted and binds up their wounds.
Psalm 147:3

*Do not let unwholesome talk come out of your mouths, but only
what is helpful for building others up according to their areas, that
it may benefit those who listen. Ephesians 4:29*

Give and it shall be given to you; good measure, pressed
down, and shaken together, and running over, shall men give
into your bosom. Luke 6:38 (KJV)

*And be not conformed to this world; but be ye transformed by the
renewing of your mind, that ye may prove what is that good, and
acceptable, and perfect will of God. Romans 12:2 (KJV)*

In everything set them an example by doing what is good.
Titus 2:7

*When pride comes, then comes disgrace, but with humility comes
wisdom. Proverbs 11:2*

If it is possible, as far as it depends on you, live at peace with
everyone. Romans 12:18

*For everyone who exalts himself will be humbled, and he who
humbles himself will be exalted. Luke 14:11*

May the God of Peace, who through the blood of the
eternal covenant brought back from the dead our
Lord Jesus, that great shepherd of the sheep, equip you
with everything good for doing his will, and may he work
in us what is pleasing to him through Jesus Christ,
to whom be glory for ever and ever. Amen.
Hebrews 13:20

Acknowledgements

Grace Upon Grace is a book about acknowledging the people, events, and graces that worked together to make up my life story. Inside the book, more than 75 people have been mentioned by name. I am grateful for each of those and many others who had a role in making me who I am.

My family has been the greatest grace of my life. I hope this book provided you a glimpse into how amazingly loving and supportive they have been, even in our darkest hours. Thank you, Jennifer and Kevin, Kim and Huntleigh, and Michael and Kelley. You are the people who inspire me.

I also want to thank Madeline's family. You were thrown into an exceedingly challenging situation and embraced me and my love for your mom. Thank you, Ashley, David, Melissa, Michael, and Brittany.

As with any book, there are several people in the background who provided information, suggestions, and encouragement to continue on with the complex and difficult task of creating a book.

My sister Evelyn Addis helped me fill in the blanks on the date, time, and sequence of many events that were emotional and foggy in my memory. Without her detail for times and dates, many important events would have been forgotten or inaccurate.

Steve Williford is a terrific editor. He provided me feedback and suggestions for improvement. His vision of the book helped enhance it from a family history book to one that a reader could apply to their own life.

Melissa Farr has been my graphic designer for almost 20 years. She is the best and is an absolute delight to work with. She did a really good job making the book look and feel like a friendly read.

My wife, Madeline, read about five drafts of the manuscript. Each time she provided some input and spice that helped make the book more personal. Thank you for your patience!

As I mentioned early in the book, the main purpose of my story is to make you more aware of the grace upon grace in your life. I hope that we have worked together to accomplish that goal.

Other Books by David Cottrell

---

136 Effective Presentation Tips

175 Ways to Get More Done in Less Time

Birdies, Pars, and Bogeys: Leadership Lessons From the Links

Becoming the Obvious Choice

David Cottrell's Collection of Favorite Quotations

Escape From Management Land

Indispensable! Becoming the Obvious Choice in Business and in Life

Listen Up, Leader!

Listen Up, Teacher!

Listen Up! Customer Service

LeaderShift … Making leadership everyone's business

Leadership Courage

Memos to Managers

Monday Morning Choices: 12 Powerful Ways to Go From Everyday to Extraordinary

Monday Morning Customer Service

Monday Morning Leadership: 8 Mentoring Sessions You Can't Afford to Miss

Monday Morning Leadership for Kids

Monday Morning Mentoring: Ten Lessons to Guide You Up the Ladder

Second Quarter: Get the Most Out of Life's Toughest Times

The First Two Rules of Leadership: Don't Be Stupid. Don't Be a Jerk.

The Leadership Secrets of Santa Claus

The Manager's Coaching Handbook

The Manager's Communication Handbook

The Manager's Conflict Resolution Handbook

The Next Level

The Nature of Excellence

Time! 105 Ways to Get More Done Every Workday

Tuesday Morning Coaching: Eight Simple Truths to Boost Your Career and Your Life

Winners Always Quit! Seven Pretty Good Habits You Can Swap for Really Great Results

Available at **CornerStoneLeadership.com**,
Amazon.com, or your local bookstore.

About the Author

David Cottrell is president and CEO of CornerStone Leadership. He is a premier authority on leadership and has worked with many of today's most successful organizations, mentoring leaders to peak performance.

Before founding CornerStone, David held leadership positions with Xerox and FedEx and led the successful turnaround of a Chapter 11 company. He has shared his leadership philosophy and lessons in keynotes and workshops with more than 400,000 leaders worldwide.

David has authored more than 25 books, read by millions of readers, including the perennial best-selling *Monday Morning Leadership*.

David can be reached at www.CornerStoneLeadership.com

CornerStone
Leadership Institute

www.CornerStoneLeadership.com

www.CornerStoneLeadership.com